the vegetaria

the vegetarian traveler

A GUIDE TO EATING GREEN IN OVER 200 COUNTRIES

BRYAN GEON

Warwick Publishing
Toronto Chicago
www.warwickgp.com

Previously published as *Speaking Vegetarian*

Warwick Edition © 2000 by Bryan Geon

We acknowledge the financial support of the Government of Canada through the Book Publishing Industry Development Program for our publishing activities.

ISBN: 1-894020-85-5

Published by **Warwick Publishing**
162 John Street, Toronto, ON M5V 2E5 Canada

Distributed in Canada by **General Distribution Services Ltd.**
325 Humber College Blvd., Toronto, ON M9W 7C3

Distributed in the U.S. by **LCP Group**
1436 West Randolph Street, Chicago, Illinois 60607

Design: Kimberley Young
Front cover photo: www.comstock.com
Author photo: Karen Smith Geon

Printed in Canada

table of contents

4. NORTH AFRICA AND THE MIDDLE EAST 109

Acknowledgments

The completion of this book would have been utterly impossible without the assistance of scores of individuals who gave selflessly of their knowledge and their time. Particular thanks are due to the following people and organizations:

Philippe Accilien, Razvan Adam, Ummul Ahmad, Ishfaq Ahmed, Lars Andersen, Mike Andrejka, Nyma Ardalan, Kagan Arik, Hatice Atkim, Marius Baciu, Chris Barbee, Boban Basic, Emil Beli, Jan-Tom Bellos, Burhan Belturan, Adolphe Bernotas, Samir Bhagwat, Peter Bjoern, Alison Brooks, Retha Calitz, Michael Charney, Niladri Chatterjee, Cheng-Yong Lee, Willard Chikavumba, Seng Chiu, Cory Clark, Katherine Cooper, Oliver Corff, Irma DeMaio, Baru Diakite, Rossen Dimitrov, Jone Dvauhimasi, Pavel Dvorak, EDUCA, Robyn Fass, Dennis Fiddle, Dana Foote, Jerry Frontosa, Terence Fu, Shakashe (Conrad) Gaopalelwe, Angela Gelli, Russ Gibbons, Vincenzo Giordano, Muhammad Hamid, Meghan Hays, Victor Herlianto, Michelle Higuchi, Alina Holgate, Nadeem Jamali, Vojin Janjic, Jianho Wang, Mahndra Joshi, Gillian Kahn, Sasho Kalajdzievski, Abdul Kamer, Byungsik Kang, Matoize Katsande, Tamás Kovács, John Kozyn, Christos Ktenas, Tatyana Kulyabina, Michal Kurmanowicz, Victor Hugo Lane, Lesotho Cash Stores (Qacha's Nek), Daniela Lessa, Ales Lipuscek, Greg Liu, Gabriela Lopes da Cruz, Josep Lopez Besora, Jack Lupic, José Machicao, Michael Martin, Yoko Masuzawa, Christy Mbonu, Sanath Meegalla, Francis Najarian, Samir Nassar, Eric Natanael, Tshimis Ngalamulume, Candide Nsabimbona, Jamie O'Connell, Hans-Henrik Ohlsen, William Omondi, Neven Orhanovic, Xavier Ormaetxea, Ana Osterman, Atul Paki, John Pandis, Hyun Ok Park, Mohammed Pasban, Patrick Patterson, Anne Paulin, Anna Pezacki, Homme Piest, Michael Piscopo, Fernand Poukie-Kono, Honoré Albert Rakotoarivony, Pierre-Michel Rameau, Gilbert Ramirez, Jr., Joe Reis, Cathy Relang, Markus Rieder, Pierre Rossi, Vincent Schonau, Fiona Scorgie, Uday Sekar, Mini Shambe, Asad Abu Shark, Ashok Shrestha, Cynthia Smith, Koobaï Souaïbou, Vladimir Stoyanovski, Daina Stukuls, John Subaykan, Anita Subramaniam, Pat Srinivas, Saurabh Thapliyal, Heang Tin, Todd Tocci, Svein Valfells, Peter Vanatko, Jacquelien Van Stekelenburg, Natasia Veikune, Kiril Vidimce, Zeenad Abdul Wahid, Kesang Wangdi, Andrea Williams-Stewart, N. Wongsurawat, Heidemarie Workman, Daniel Woubishet, Katy

Youel, Muhammed Zaman, and Gayle Zilber, as well as to the diplomatic personnel and other individuals who asked to remain anonymous. Special thanks go to my wife, Karen Smith Geon, for her unflagging support and assistance.

Introduction

Dining is one of the great pleasures of travel. Besides its obvious function of basic nourishment, eating serves as a way to experience a country and its culture through its food. Upscale restaurants in major tourist destinations usually have menus in English; however, off the beaten tourist track or in less expensive restaurants, menus in English are rare. Sometimes no menus are available in any language, and in many countries English-speakers are equally scarce. It is always a surprise and often a treat to order from a foreign-language menu, waiting to see what mystery dish arrives at the table.

Unfortunately for vegetarians, in most countries that mystery dish is likely to contain meat. Most pocket phrasebooks do not address the problem, and usually contain translations for quaint but worthless phrases like, "Are traditional breaded pork cutlets available in this establishment?" Those who choose not to eat meat have traditionally been limited to four options: (1) buy and prepare one's own food, avoiding restaurants; (2) eat meat if it comes; (3) eat only dishes one can see in advance, and hope no meat is concealed within; (4) stay home.

The intent of this book is to make it possible for vegetarian travelers to communicate their particular dietary preferences virtually anywhere in the world. It is not intended to make you sound anything like a native speaker of the languages featured. Speaking even a few halting phrases in the language of the country you are visiting is a sign of respect, and is bound to win you goodwill, even if your diet puzzles the person you address. Unfortunately, the phrases contained in this book cannot solve every problem. Even if your wish for meatless dishes gets across, some people will misunderstand the nature of vegetarianism or will consider you deprived and try to foist meat upon you for your own good. Unfortunately, no phrasebook can help overcome cultural and personality differences of this sort. You are on your own as a vegetarian diplomat.

It is impossible to include every one of the thousands of human languages spoken throughout the world. Instead, the book contains phrases in the official or major languages for every country. The omission of minor languages should not be taken as a sign of cultural insensitivity, but rather as a concession to pragmatism: The book is much more portable, most people speak a national tongue at least as a second language, and even in cases where you cannot speak directly to a local, someone nearby probably speaks the national language and will be able to translate for you.

This book does not adopt a single definition of "vegetarian." In most cases, it allows the reader to mix and match phrases to communicate exactly what someone does or does not eat. Some people who consider themselves vegetarians only avoid red meat, while vegans avoid animal products entirely. Other travelers normally eat meat at home, but avoid it while traveling because of unsanitary conditions in some less-developed countries. This book is designed for all of these types of "vegetarians," and for everyone in between. A reference to fish, chicken, or cheese is not intended to offend strict vegetarians. (In any case, if the mere thought of someone eating any kind of flesh or dairy product truly offends you, there are very few places in the world you can safely visit.)

The chapters are organized by region of the world, and subdivided by country. Indexes list countries and languages. Each country's listing first contains a brief synopsis of the general availability of meatless entrees in that country. The listing is not intended to be comprehensive, and does not list every common vegetarian dish. In addition, the availability of vegetarian food may vary significantly from one region of a country to the next. The second part of the listing contains translations and phonetic pronunciations (or cross-references to them) for phrases a vegetarian might use, in the language or languages of that country. And all listings contain a translation for the most important phrase of all: Thank you.

Readers of this book probably will find it most useful in restaurants, food stalls, or snack shacks. However, it is possible that you might be invited to a home for a meal. Such situations present the polite, culturally sensitive vegetarian with a dilemma. In many countries, it is incredibly rude to refuse food in a home, regardless of your normal dietary habits. Especially in poorer households, your hosts may be insulted because they think you are patronizingly trying to spare them the expense of buying meat or consider their offering to be beneath you. At the very least, eat as much as you can of any meatless food offered. You can try to pantomime that eating meat will make you sick (which it might) or that you are allergic. However, a badly done pantomime is likely to be even more insulting that leaving the food on the plate! Alternatively, of course, you can simply eat the meat. It is a matter for your own conscience.

In many parts of the world, vegetarians (as well as most locals) may be restricted to a diet that is heavy on starch and light on vegetables or fruit. This problem is particularly acute in less-developed countries in Africa, Asia, and Latin America. While in the short term such a diet will probably not have any significant adverse health effects, travelers who will be gone for a substantial length of time may wish to take vitamins or other nutritional supplements. It may also be a good idea to take along high-protein foods such as peanut butter.

It is also an unfortunate fact of life in some countries that the very foods that are most attractive to many vegetarian travelers—salads, unpeeled fruit, and uncooked vegetables—can lead to serious discomfort, or even serious health problems, if they not properly cleaned and prepared. These otherwise enticing items may harbor a variety of unpleasant beasties that will swiftly ruin your journey if ingested. Unless you can be sure that the produce has been cleaned appropriately, it is better to eat only vegetables that have been thoroughly (and recently) cooked, and fruits that can be peeled.

Finally, enjoy your travels! With this book as a tool, it should be possible to get meatless food almost anywhere. While in some cases your diet may be limited to grains, starches, and legumes (in other words, the food of the poor in that country), you are more likely to encounter delicious and unusual vegetarian dishes. Eat with pleasure—and remember to call the airline in advance of your departure to reserve a vegetarian meal.

Phrases and Pronunciation
The phrases on this book have been standardized. Although the literal meaning of a word or phrase in the original language may differ from the English words, the general meaning will be the same. (For example, the sentence "I would like something without ___" might be best translated as "I want to eat a dish without ___ please," or "I wish to eat food that does not contain ___.")

The phrases and words have been presented with blanks in appropriate places so that you can mix and match words depending on what specifically you do or do not eat. ("I do not eat ___"; "I eat ___.") In some languages, the form of a noun like "meat" will vary depending on how it is used; in such cases, the appropriate version of the word is the one found immediately below the sentence you are using.

The phonetic pronunciations provided have been made as simple as possible within the bounds of reasonable accuracy. You are unlikely ever to be mistaken for a native speaker, and in some cases the pronunciation will sound awkward or unnatural, but you should be understood. The pronunciations should be read as if they were ordinary English words, and pronounced using standard English phonetics. Syllables in all capital letters should be STRESSED. A few important sounds are not self-evident, or have no obvious English equivalent. These are:

zh   "zh" denotes the sound of "s" in pleasure, or the "zh" of *Dr. Zhivago.*

kh   the bold "kh" is the guttural sound of German "ch", or the "ch" sound in the Scottish *loch*. When properly done, it sounds as if you are bringing up pleghm from the back of your throat.

ng   the bold "ng" is pronounced as the middle "ng" in *singing*; the g is not strongly pronounced.

n   bold "n" is not really an "n" at all. This symbol is used to indicate that the preceding vowel sound is nasalized, as in French. (Try saying the vowel as if you were speaking through your nose.)

A few other sounds have more than one possible pronunciation in English. The intended sounds for the purposes of this book are set out below:

g   "g" is always a hard sound, as in *go,* not the soft g of *giant.*

oh   "oh" is a long o sound, as in *go.*

aw   "aw" is always pronounced as in *saw.*

ow   "ow" is pronounced like the exclamation of pain, or as in *cow.*

uh   "uh" is a short u sound, as in *nut.*

eye   "eye", or "consonant-ye" combinations like "dye" or "rye", are pronounced as a long i, as in *my.*

A Note on Tonal Languages

Many east Asian languages are tonal. In tonal languages, the meaning of a word can vary depending on the tone, or pitch, in which it is spoken. It is difficult to learn tones from a book (and not particularly easy to learn them from a live person). However, the closest analogy is to reading music—higher tones are at higher pitches, just like musical notes. In the pronunciations given in this book, three lines of text are used. The line on which the written translation occurs shows where middle pitch should be; words on the line above are high tones, words on the line below are low tones.

For example:

If the sentence ended here: this is the **middle** tone $^{\text{this one }\textbf{high}}$ $_{\text{and this }\textbf{low}}$.

There is no absolute standard of high and low tone; the pitches are relative to your ordinary way of speaking.

Individual words can also change pitch. Changing pitch is indicated by one of four symbols:

↗   This symbol shows that the word has a rising tone. A rising tone is said as if a question were being asked, or as if one were singing notes that were rising in pitch. This symbol is placed immediately in front of the phonetic pronunciation of the word.

↘   This symbol shows that the word has a falling tone. A falling tone is said as if one were emphasizing a word, or descending downwards in the musical scale. This symbol is placed immediately in front of the phonetic pronunciation of the word.

^   This symbol over a letter within the phonetic pronunciation of a word (e.g., â) indicates that the word rises in tone, then drops.

˘   This symbol over a letter within the phonetic pronunciation of a word (e.g., ĕ) indicates that the tone falls, then rises.

Although proper pitch is important for comprehension, even if you botch things up superbly, you will probably still be understood in the context of the sentence. (You might also unintentionally cause guffaws among your listeners when you say something like, "I do not eat umbrellas.")

North America

The United States and Canada have the most diverse populations in the world. Native speakers of every language in this book (and several hundred more besides) are found in both countries; the cuisines of a hundred nations are served in restaurants throughout the cities and towns of North America. However, when people from other parts of the world think of "American" food (or Canadian food, if they think of it at all), they are likely to think of quickie hamburgers or fried chicken. Fast-food franchises seem to be North America's contribution to world cuisine.

In reality, North American food is much more complex and interesting than the global burger barons let on. Every region has its local specialties, including a number of meatless delicacies—at the very least, desserts are usually vegetarian, if not vegan. A kaleidoscope of ethnic restaurants can be found in cities, and sometimes in the most unlikely rural areas: Chinese food in the Wyoming desert, Ethiopian food in small-town Michigan, Mexican food on the Saskatchewan prairie. Test the phrases in this book on restaurateurs who come from other countries (although you should not try to impress a date at a fancy French restaurant).

English-speaking visitors from outside North America may find not only that many North American dishes have odd names that do not betray their contents, but also that common vegetarian ingredients have unfamiliar names. The most prominent example is "corn," a term that North Americans use to refer specifically to maize. Other examples include peppers (capsicum), eggplant (aubergine), zucchini (courgette), and squash, the name for a whole group of vegetables that include courgette, marrow, and pumpkin. When in doubt, ask for a description of the item in question; most North Americans will be happy (perhaps overly so) to explain.

The United States

In the United States, most vegetarians—and consequently most specialist vegetarian or veggie-friendly restaurants—are concentrated in the cities of the Northeast and along the West Coast. Resort areas and college towns across the country are also fertile ground. However, with perseverance it is possible to get meatless meals anywhere in the country. Salad bars and all-you-can-eat buffets, while of wildly uneven quality, are common even in the solidly carnivorous Plains states. Small-town restaurants are often happy to make vegetable or cheese sandwiches, salads, or even plain steamed vegetables on request—although you may get a sidelong suspicious glance if you state outright that you are a vegetarian.

Although **English** obviously predominates, the United States has no official language. Languages of every country on earth are spoken here, especially in large urban areas. Some languages are especially common in particular regions: Spanish is widely spoken in California, the Southwest and Florida, as well as in the urban Northeast; French is used in parts of Louisiana and northern New England; German, Polish, and the Scandinavian languages form the linguistic heritage of many Midwesterners; Asian languages are common in urban areas on the West Coast; and in ethnic enclaves throughout the United States, people speak in the tongues and dialects of their native lands.

Canada

The vegetarian demography of Canada is much like that of its southern neighbor: Urban areas in Ontario, Quebec and western Canada have the heaviest concentrations of vegetarians (as they do of Canadians in general). Vegetarian offerings are also quite easy to find in resort areas such as Banff. Elsewhere, the vegetarian's burden is heavier. Fish still figures heavily in the diet of the Maritime provinces, while the prairie provinces of Alberta, Saskatchewan, and Manitoba are hardly less carnivorous than their counterparts south of the border. Even so, meatless entrees can be found in restaurants almost anywhere in Canada—even in such an unlikely locale as Whitehorse, the far-flung capital of the Yukon Territory.

Canada's linguistic picture is complicated by the sometimes uneasy coexistence of two official languages, **English** and **French** (p. 66). English is the native tongue of most Canadians. French is spoken in Quebec, and in scattered communities in other provinces. Although Montreal is largely bilingual, in other areas of Quebec English is not widely spoken and by law all signs must be in French. The varieties of French spoken in Canada are quite different from continental French, and visitors may have a difficult time understanding the spoken version. French-speaking visitors should still be understood.

Thanks to a recent influx of immigrants, Cantonese and other East Asian languages are very common in Vancouver.

Latin America and the Caribbean

Latin America and the Caribbean Islands are a choice destination for sun-seeking tourists from northern latitudes. Unfortunately, many visitors know little about the cuisines and languages of these countries. Most people in North America, Western Europe, and Australia are familiar with the so-called "Mexican" food purveyed at fast-food restaurants or in kitschy fake cantinas, but the nachos, fajitas, and enchiladas served in such establishments bear little resemblance to the dishes served in Mexico. The many styles of Mexican cuisine are in turn very different from the cuisines of nations further south or east.

Of course, the cuisine in this part of the world shares some common elements. The staple meal in many Latin American and Caribbean countries is rice in combination with some form of beans—black beans, kidney beans, or pigeon peas. Unfortunately for vegetarians, the beans are often cooked in lard. In fact, lard is used in many fried foods, and is sometimes even added to butter. Furthermore, some apparently innocuous soups and stews contain bacon or ham for flavor.

The good news is that Latin America and the Caribbean feature a rich variety of regional cuisines and local dishes, not all of which rely on meat. Some dishes display the influence of immigrant groups, such as East Indians in the Caribbean or Italians in parts of South America. Other dishes work wonders with indigenous foods and local methods of cooking and spicery. Wherever you go, it is worth seeking out local dishes. If you are searching for a change of dietary pace, remember that Chinese restaurants are found throughout Latin America and the Caribbean and usually serve one or more vegetarian dishes.

Language
There are hundreds of indigenous languages spoken in this area of the world.

The vast majority of these languages have relatively few speakers; in other cases, a given language may have many dialects, each of which is spoken only in a small region. In most (but not all) cases, someone who speaks a country's primary or official language will be on hand if translation is required. For reasons of space, economy, and utility, this book reluctantly omits most of these languages.

Spanish dominates the hemisphere. Because it is used in almost 20 of the countries listed below, it is presented here first. There are some differences in pronunciation from one country to another, but the standard pronunciations below should be understood by Spanish speakers anywhere.

NOTE: Throughout much of Spanish-speaking Latin America, the word for meat (*carne*) is typically understood to refer only to red meat, and sometimes only to beef. As a consequence, you may need to be very specific about what you do or do not eat.

Spanish

I would like something without _____.	Quisiera comer algo sin _____.	kee-see-YAIR-uh co-MAIR AHL-goh seen _____.
We would like something without _____.	Quisieramos comer algo sin _____.	kee-see-YAIR-ah-mohs co-MAIR AHL-goh seen _____.
I do not eat _____.	No como _____.	noh KOH-moh _____.
I eat _____ and _____.	Como _____ y _____.	KOH-moh _____ ee _____.
meat	carne	KAR-nay
pork	puerco	PWEHR-koh
chicken	pollo	POY-yoh
fish	pescado	peh-SKAH-doh

eggs	huevos	WAY-bohs
cheese	queso	KAY-soh
lard (sometimes also used to refer to butter or margarine)	manteca	mahn-TAY-kah
I am a vegetarian. (male speaker)	Soy vegetariano.	soy vay-hay-tah-ree-AH-noh
I am a vegetarian. (female speaker)	Soy vegetariana.	soy vay-hay-tah-ree-AH-nah
Please	Por favor	pohr fah-BOHR
Thank you	Gracias	GRAH-see-ahs

A. MEXICO AND CENTRAL AMERICA

Mexico and the Central American nations benefit or suffer, depending on one's point of view, from the proximity of the United States. One side effect of the resulting spillover of North American culture is the proliferation of egregious North American fast-food establishments and chain restaurants in major cities throughout this part of the world. However, there is still a strong current of traditionalism, even in matters of cuisine. As elsewhere in Latin America, rice and beans are staple foods and are served with abandon (and you may indeed wish to abandon them eventually), but there are also national and regional specialties waiting to be discovered—seek and you shall find.

Belize
Belize has a remarkably cosmopolitan heritage, but unfortunately Belizean cuisine does not fully reflect this diversity. Excellent fresh seafood is available, but true vegetarians will find slim pickings. Vegetables are fairly uncommon and usually canned, although good tropical fruit is widely available. Rice, beans, and plantains (often fried in lard) are standard. Some resorts and restaurants that cater to foreign tourists offer more variety, and generally have one or more options for vegetarians. If you crave Asian cuisine, there are Chinese and Indian restaurants in the larger towns; these may be the best options for vegetarians outside the resort areas.

English is the official language, but most people speak a Creole patois at home (although they generally can also speak standard English). Spanish (p. 26) is spoken in the north and west. Mayan languages, Garífuna (the language of the Black Caribs), and a German dialect (spoken by Mennonites) are also used in some areas of the country.

Costa Rica
Costa Ricans love meat; fortunately for vegetarian visitors, they also eat other foods from time to time. Fresh seafood is available for pesco-vegetarians everywhere along the coasts. Restaurants offering various European cuisines, as well as North American fast-food standards, are scattered throughout the main cities. Pizza, pasta, and salads are particularly common, and there are Chinese restaurants everywhere. Bakeries serve up tasty meatless treats (but

beware—some baked goods contain lard). Costa Rica also produces several varieties of cheese, so cheese sandwiches are an option for non-vegans. And of course, rice and beans can be found everywhere in the country.

Spanish (p. 26) is spoken throughout the country. English is spoken in some communities along the Caribbean coast.

El Salvador
The capital city, San Salvador, has a few specifically vegetarian restaurants, and a number of Italian and other European-style restaurants that serve some meatless dishes. Outside the city, as in rural areas throughout Central America, rice and beans are standard. *Pupusas*, tortillas stuffed with various ingredients and fried (sometimes in lard), are unique to El Salvador and are available throughout the country. While the fillings are usually beef, pork, or chicken, it is possible to find interesting meatless varieties that contain cheese, black beans, or pumpkin.

Spanish (p. 26) is the national language. A relatively small number of people, mainly in the highland areas, speak indigenous languages.

Guatemala
While few Guatemalans are vegetarians, the constant stream of gringo visitors has resulted in the establishment of a number of vegetarian restaurants in Guatemala City and other well-touristed areas. Guatemala City also features an array of international cuisines (especially Italian restaurants with pizza and pasta), with the usual sprinkling of Chinese restaurants. In the countryside, rice, beans, eggs, and tortillas are the staples, often served with chicken. Banana, coconut, and fried plantains are common ingredients on the Caribbean coast. Fish-eaters will find that fresh fish is easily available on both coasts and in many inland locations.

Spanish (p. 26) is the official language. Many Indians in the Guatemalan highlands speak one of many indigenous languages as a native tongue, and some speak no Spanish at all (although a Spanish-speaker usually can be found nearby).

Honduras
Both main cities (Tegucigalpa and San Pedro Sula) have a few vegetarian

restaurants, as well as some restaurants that serve European-style food. The standard ensemble of rice, beans, and tortillas is found everywhere, in or out of the cities. Chicken is the most common accompaniment in inland areas; fish is usual on the coast. Coconut is used extensively on the Caribbean coast, where it is used in making bread. There are Chinese restaurants in some smaller towns, as well as in large cities. The Bay Islands in the Caribbean, off the north coast, receive large numbers of tourists, and many island restaurants serve meatless dishes.

Spanish (p. 26) is the national language. English is the first language of some communities along the north coast and of most natives of the Bay Islands. Garífuna-speaking Black Caribs live in some coastal villages in the north.

Mexico

Contrary to the perceptions of many visitors, Mexico has a highly varied regional cuisine (although as in most Latin American countries rice and beans are staples almost everywhere). Indeed, the variety of Mexican cuisine can pose special problems for vegetarian travelers: Furry jungle animals are consumed in the Yucatan and the far south, and iguanas are sometimes eaten along the west coast. While pork, chicken, and beef are frequently used, there are many dishes that contain cheese instead of meat, or that feature wonderful *salsas* with vegetables and grains or potatoes. (Beware of lard, however). Fish-eaters will be happy virtually anywhere along Mexico's thousands of miles of coast.

Vegetarianism has started to become something of a fad among the middle and upper classes, and there are a growing number of vegetarian restaurants in the cities and resort areas. Some restaurants in these areas also serve a variety of international dishes, including pizza and pasta. The standard array of North American fast-food nightmares can be found in most regions of the country. Chinese restaurants are found in Mexican towns, sometimes in unlikely places such as the middle of the Sonoran Desert.

Spanish (p. 26) is the official language. Mexico has dozens of different Indian groups, each with its own language; some 20 languages are spoken in the Yucatan alone. Many Indians speak no Spanish, although someone who speaks Spanish can usually be found within hailing distance.

Nicaragua

The former Sandinista regime made a concerted effort to promote soya as an alternative source of protein. As a result, vegetarian restaurants serving soy dishes are scattered around Nicaragua, although they are not necessarily well patronized. In rural areas, volunteer organizations use soya to reduce malnutrition. (Most locals, however, would still rather have meat.) Despite the insurgence of soy, rice and beans are still the main foods for most Nicaraguans. North American, Italian, and other European-style dishes are available in the cities. There are also Chinese restaurants in most Nicaraguan cities.

Spanish (p. 26) is the official language. English is the primary language in some villages along the east coast, while Indians in the remote, rural northeast speak indigenous tongues.

Panama

Panama sometimes bills itself as the crossroads of the world. Unfortunately, the world seems to eat a lot of meat. As one would expect of a country with two seacoasts so close together and a canal down the middle, fish is also quite common, so pesco-vegetarians will be content. Tropical fruit is excellent and can be found everywhere. Traffic from the Panama Canal ensures the presence of a wide variety of international cuisines, including the inevitable Chinese restaurants, as well as the occasional exclusively vegetarian eatery. Despite Panama's relatively cosmopolitan atmosphere, rice and beans remain the staples for many people, especially outside the cities. In parts of the Darién jungle, it may be very difficult to find non-meat dishes.

Spanish is the national language. Due to the U.S. presence in the former Canal Zone, many Panamanians speak English; some native Anglophone black Panamanians live on the Caribbean coast. Many Indians in the Darién speak indigenous languages and do not know Spanish.

B. THE CARIBBEAN

Rice and peas (pigeon peas or kidney beans, sometimes made with lard or pork) are the Caribbean staples—the island counterpart to mainland Latin America's rice and beans. The Caribbean islands have a diverse cultural heritage—in addition to the tourists that invade every winter from North America, immigrants have come from Africa, Europe, and Asia—and there is surprising variation in cooking styles within and between islands. Thanks to migrants from South Asia, on many of the English-speaking islands one can find *roti*, a thin pancake wrapped around a spicy filling. Usually roti is filled with meat, but some vegetarian varieties contain lentils or vegetables. As one might expect of islands, seafood figures heavily in Caribbean cuisine. There are also plenty of unusual tropical fruits and vegetables to try. Unfortunately, on some islands local restaurants are difficult to find, and hotel and resort restaurants may offer the only sustenance. Such restaurants often, but not always, offer at least one meatless dish.

Antigua and Barbuda
In local restaurants, there are peas and rice a-plenty. Roti and curries are common, if not always vegetarian, and West Indian–style seafood is found everywhere. In the hotel restaurants, "international" cuisine is the rule, and vegetarian entrees may not always be available.
   English is the official language.

Bahamas
The nation comprises hundreds of islands, and consequently fish and shellfish feature heavily in the local cuisine. Conch in various forms is peddled everywhere, and boiled fish with grits (displaying the culinary influence of the American South) is a staple. For true vegetarians, options are few. Peas and rice are as common as they are elsewhere in the Caribbean, and peas are often made into a soup. Unfortunately, the soup usually contains meat for flavoring. The truly desperate can ask local restaurants to prepare special meals, or can try tourist restaurants, which often serve pasta or pizza. Hotels usually offer salads or other light meatless dishes.
   English is the official language. Many Bahamians speak a Creole dialect among themselves.

Barbados

Barbados offers limited vegetarian options, although fish-eaters will be happy. Flying fish is the national dish, and the island is strewn with British-style fish-and-chip joints. Curries are occasionally available, although they are not often vegetarian. Roti is available in some areas, and a diligent search can turn up interesting local specialties like pumpkin fritters, coconut pie, and cou-cou (okra and cornmeal/ground maize). Otherwise, hotel and resort restaurants generally serve or can specially prepare some meatless dish.

English is spoken everywhere on this small island.

The British Islands

Anguilla is celebrated for its seafood. (Because the name means "eel," this is not surprising.) Shellfish is particularly renowned. Strict vegetarians will find that, unlike on some Caribbean islands, fresh vegetables are common here.

Bermuda, while not physically in the Caribbean, has Caribbean-style traditional cooking; rice and peas and fish dishes are found in local establishments. The tourist restaurants and resorts mainly serve "international" cuisine, with vegetarian dishes sometimes available.

In the **British Virgin Islands**, most restaurants are expensive, tourist-oriented establishments serving seafood and "international" cuisine, and are not really geared toward vegetarians. Local food, which follows the typical Caribbean model, is usually not offered in restaurants.

On the **Cayman Islands**, traditional food is increasingly difficult to find, but once found it generally follows the standard Caribbean pattern. One variation is that sea turtles are raised for human consumption on Grand Cayman, so a heaping dish of endangered reptile is alarmingly easy to find at local restaurants or in resort dining rooms. Several of the resort hotel kitchens offer meatless entrees.

Montserrat formerly had some of the best fresh fruit and vegetables in the Caribbean. However, the volcano that has devastated the island and caused the evacuation of most of the population has changed the food situation drastically. Visitors to Montserrat today are unlikely to find many vegetarian options, or indeed many food options of any kind.

The **Turks and Caicos Islands** are located just south of the Bahamas and have virtually identical food. Seafood is king here.

All these islands are British possessions. **English** is the language of choice.

Cuba

Cubans love pork, chicken, and seafood. However, thanks to Castro's policies and the economic effects of the U.S. embargo, most Cubans are currently unwilling vegetarians. Fresh vegetables generally are rare, although sweet potatoes and other root vegetables are relatively common. Fruit is often available. Unlike most Caribbean islanders, Cubans favor black beans instead of pigeon peas. Restaurants, limited in number and tightly regulated under the Communist regime, are slowly liberalizing, but some of the best food on the island is still only available in informal (and officially illegal) family-run restaurants.

Spanish (p. 26) is spoken throughout the country.

Dominica

Goat, chicken, pork, and seafood are all common. So is pondfood: giant frog legs (mountain chicken) is the national dish. For those who eschew, rather than chew, amphibians, all is not lost. Some hotel restaurants offer vegetable platters, and a few rastafarians live on the island. Rice and peas are found here as elsewhere in the Caribbean, and fresh fruit is both abundant and excellent.

English is the official language, but most islanders speak a French patois among themselves.

Dominican Republic

Santo Domingo has one or two vegetarian restaurants, but in general it is fairly difficult to get meatless food. Beef, pork, tripe, and goat, sometimes in the form of stew, are all standard, but rice and beans usually accompany the main dish and can of course be ordered separately. Some interesting vegetable pastries are available, and pizza and pasta can be found in towns. North American–style chain restaurants are found in the cities and offer the sole advantage of serving safe-to-eat salads. In beach resort areas, hotels and restaurants sometimes offer vegetarian dishes. If you cook for yourself, you are likely to find that the quality of fruits and vegetables is generally higher in the Dominican Republic than elsewhere in the Caribbean.

Spanish (p. 26) is the national language.

The French Islands

The French influence is obvious on these islands—*patisseries, boulangeries,* and crepe shops are found everywhere, and provide tasty meat-free carbohydrates.

Guadeloupe and **Martinique** have a vibrant Creole culture, and traditional Creole kitchens (which, unfortunately, emphasize meat and seafood dishes) are found alongside elegant bistros.

St. Barthélemy (often called St. Barts) and **St. Martin** display less Creole influence, and traditional European cuisine, particularly French cuisine, is prevalent in restaurants.

French (p. 66) is the official language. On Guadeloupe and Martinique, most islanders speak a Creole dialect among themselves. English is not commonly spoken.

Grenada

Grenada is famous for its nutmeg. Unfortunately, when consumed alone in large quantities, nutmeg is mildly hallucinogenic and causes nausea. It is therefore wise to seek out other sustenance. Meat and fish dishes are the focus, but vegetarian roti is sometimes an option. There are also Italian restaurants that serve pizza and pasta. Of course, peas and rice are always available, as is fabulous fresh fruit. Hotel restaurants present a final, and less than ideal, choice; most have salads, but more substantial vegetarian dishes may not be on the menu.

English is the official language, but many islanders speak a French-African patois among themselves.

Haiti

Haiti is the poorest country in the Western Hemisphere, and consequently the average Haitian does not eat meat regularly. Rice with kidney beans and plantains is the staple meal. Some interesting variations exist, such as *riz djon-djon* (rice with black mushrooms). However, Haitians love meat when they can get it, so restaurants do not focus on meatless dishes. Fish is consumed along the coast, and there are a few French and Italian restaurants in Port-au-Prince (as well as a smattering of American fast food restaurants).

French (p. 66) is the official language. However, most Haitians cannot speak French, and **Haitian Creole** is the *lingua franca.* Even the educated upper classes speak Creole at home.

Haitian Creole

Because Haitian Creole is largely an oral language, usage can vary significantly from one region to another. The phrases below are commonly used constructions that should be generally understood.

I would like something without _____.	Mwen vle manje san _____.	mwahn vlay mahnj sahn _____.
We would like something without _____.	Nou vle manje san _____.	noo vlay mahnj san _____.
I do not eat _____.	Mwen pa manje _____.	mwahn pah mahnj _____.
I eat _____ and _____.	Mwen manje _____ ak _____.	mwahn mahnj _____ ehk _____.
meat	vyann	vee-AHN
chicken	poul	pool
fish	pwason	PWAH-sohn
eggs	zé	zeh
cheese	fwomaj	fwoh-MAHJ
I am a vegetarian.	Mwen se vejetaryen.	mwahn seh veh-jeh-tahr-YEHN
Please	Tanpri	tahn-PREE
Thank you	Mèsi	MEH-see

Jamaica

Jamaica has a fair number of Seventh Day Adventists, and many rastafarians are vegetarian, so vegetarianism is not an alien concept. Indeed, there are a few vegetarian restaurants serving these clienteles. Unfortunately, apart from the odd rasta and Adventist, vegetarianism is not widely practiced in Jamaica; goat and chicken are staples for almost all who can afford them or can raise them on their own. Fish is widely available, which is good news for pesco-vegetarians; so is roti. Jamaica also produces a range of interesting and unusual fruits and vegetables such as breadfruit, ackee, and peculiar types of squash (pumpkin or marrow); it is sometimes possible to find these in dishes at local restaurants. In the resort areas, hotel restaurants and other restaurants that cater specifically to tourists are reasonably likely to offer meatless dishes.

English is the official language. Although the Jamaican patois is often difficult for outsiders to fathom, *you* will usually be understood perfectly.

The Netherlands Antilles

Aruba and **Bonaire** have excellent seafood. Indonesian restaurants (which sometimes have vegetarian options) are common on both islands. **Curaçao** is an oil refinery center and is more cosmopolitan; it features a number of Latin American and European restaurants (as well as plenty of delicious petroleum). Some of the European restaurants have meatless dishes. The cuisine of **St. Maarten** has a European focus, and if none of the options there appeal to you, you can easily cross to the French side of the island for a croissant.

Saba and **St. Eustatius** (Statia) offer more traditional Caribbean food. Peas and rice with meat or fish is the order of the day.

As one would expect, **Dutch** (p. 61) is the official language of the Netherlands Antilles. However, on the "ABC" islands of Aruba, Bonaire, and Curaçao, a Creole tongue called Papiamento is the everyday language of most islanders. On St. Eustatius, St. Maarten, and Saba, English is the first language of most islanders.

St. Kitts and Nevis

In addition to the inevitable rice and peas, shellfish and breadfruit are common food items here. However, few restaurants serve local food. Hotel and resort restaurants almost invariably serve regrettable "international" cuisine, which may or may not include meatless dishes.

English is the official language.

St. Lucia
In addition to standard Caribbean fare, visitors may encounter pumpkin soup, stuffed breadfruit, and flying fish (dead and cooked rather than airborne). St. Lucia also produces wonderful tropical fruit in its lush rainforests. A few hotel restaurants and resorts offer ordinary North American or European dishes and ignore the local bounty.

English is the official language. Many islanders speak a French patois among themselves.

St. Vincent and the Grenadines
St. Vincent and the Grenadines (besides being a great potential name for a pop band) is composed of one big island and a string of small islands. As one might expect, Vincentians eat a lot of seafood. All the Caribbean standards are available here; breadfruit is a local specialty, but is difficult to find in restaurants. Fresh local tropical fruit is excellent. Many of the resorts cater to the international yachting set, and do not concern themselves with vegetarians and other lower forms of life.

English is the official language. Many islanders speak a French patois among themselves.

Trinidad and Tobago
Many Trinidadians are of Indian (Asian, not Amerindian) descent, so vegetarianism is generally understood and accepted. Although Indian restaurants are surprisingly hard to find, meatless roti and curries are not uncommon. There is also a large Chinese community in Trinidad, with the inevitable accompaniment of Chinese restaurants. The Caribbean staples are found everywhere, except in tourist hotels, which tend not to offer many vegetarian options. Trinidad's proximity to South America allows some Latin American influence to creep into the cooking.

English is the official language. Hindi (p. 180) is still spoken as a first language in many homes. Spanish (p. 26) is spoken in some districts.

The U.S. Islands

Puerto Rico is a culinary hybrid of Latin American heritage and North American cultural imperialism. The staple diet is rice and black or red beans, served with seafood, red meat, tripe, or chicken. Puerto Ricans make delicious soups, but many of these have a bone or two thrown in for flavoring. Sometimes even rice is made with bones or bits of meat. One common meatless dish is potato or another type of tuber prepared with olive oil. There are a few specialty vegetarian restaurants in and around San Juan. Puerto Rico also has many North American chain restaurants (including some with salad bars).

In the **U.S. Virgin Islands**, local cuisine is the standard Caribbean fare of rice and peas with meat or seafood. Most restaurants serve "international" cuisine and cater to tourists. Although tourist restaurants are not geared toward serving vegetarian dishes, salads, pasta, and pizza are usually available.

Since these islands are U.S. territories, **English** is widely spoken. However, in Puerto Rico the majority language is **Spanish** (p. 26). Virgin Islanders speak a lilting, Caribbean-accented English.

C. SOUTH AMERICA

South America's climate and geography varies greatly—from the glaciers and steppes of Patagonia to the Andean altiplano to the Amazon rainforest—and South American cuisine varies correspondingly. As in Central America and the Caribbean, beans with rice or another starch serve as the basis of the diet for many people, but there are many other main dishes or accompaniments, and these differ dramatically from one country or region to another.

Demography also affects the type of food you will encounter. Countries with an immigrant tradition or with a relatively large middle class, such as Argentina, Brazil, or Chile, have an international selection of foods distributed more broadly within the country. Poorer countries, such as Bolivia, offer fewer choices, and most choice that does exist is confined to cities. Nonetheless, except in the most aggressively carnivorous areas, it should be possible to find something meatless to eat.

Argentina

Argentinians consume more beef per capita than any other nationality. However, those who fear to visit this *non plus ultra* of carnivorousness should take heart; Argentina is not entirely off-limits. Buenos Aires has a burgeoning number of vegetarian restaurants (including some all-you-can-eat buffets), and in larger cities and towns most restaurants have at least one meatless entree, generally of the salad/pizza/pasta genre. There are also many grocers who specialize in macrobiotic and vegetarian food; some serve prepared meals. Because of Argentina's long history of immigration, a variety of ethnic restaurants (particularly European restaurants) exists in most cities and large towns, and it is often possible to find meatless meals at these establishments.

It becomes much more difficult to find meatless food outside cities and resort areas, and vegetarianism is less tolerated. Cheese pizza and cheese and tomato sandwiches are relatively common almost everywhere, although an exclusive diet of these items might quickly grow tiresome. The one saving grace is that the traditional Argentine meal is centered around a huge slab of beef. As a result, it is easy to give the meat a wide berth or omit it entirely. Fish-eaters will find that good seafood is usually available along the coast.

Spanish (p. 26) is the national language. There are also scattered immigrant communities which speak European or Asian languages, including German, Italian, Hebrew, and even Welsh. Some people along the Paraguayan border speak Guaraní (p. 46).

NOTE: Argentine Spanish is uniquely accented. One major difference from the pronunciations given at the beginning of this chapter is that *pollo* (chicken) is pronounced POY-zhoh, not POY-yoh.

Bolivia

Main dishes in restaurants usually contain meat, but it is usually no problem to get a meatless dish if you ask for one. Vegetable soup is common in the highlands. Although vegetarianism is not common, Bolivians on the whole appear less inclined to argue about your dietary desires than some other nationalities are; you are likely to upset them much more if you refuse to drink beer. There are vegetarian restaurants in La Paz, Santa Cruz, Potosí, and other cities and tourist centers. These cities also offer a variety of European-style food in cafes and restaurants.

Outside the cities, vegetarianism is a more difficult matter. In many poverty-stricken rural areas, people consider themselves lucky to see meat, even if you may not share their joy; they cannot imagine that those who could afford it would want to avoid meat intentionally. Nonetheless, Bolivians are hospitable and generally will try to accommodate your dietary wishes. Remember that the Incas genetically engineered the potato, and today their descendants can serve you dishes made from the miracle tuber.

Spanish (p. 26) is the main language. Bolivia has a large population of Indians, many of whom speak no Spanish. Quechua (p. 47) is spoken in some highland regions. In the far south, Guaraní (p. 46) is spoken. In the Altiplano, **Aymará** is the language most commonly spoken outside the cities.

Aymará

Note that the Aymará word for meat, aycha, *signifies all types of flesh, not just beef. The term for beef is* huaca aycha—*cow meat. Sounds appetizing, doesn't it? Aymará dialects vary considerably, but the words and phrases below are fairly standard across dialects.*

I do not eat ____.	Nayaja janiu manqueriti ____.	nye-AH-hah hah-NEE-oo mahn-kay-REE-tee ____.
meat	aycha	EYE-shah
chicken	huallpa aycha	WYE-pah EYE-shah
fish	chalhua	SHAHL-wah
eggs	cauna	HOW-nah
cheese	quisu	KEE-soo
I am a vegetarian. (Literally, "My food is what the earth produces.")	Mancanaja yapu achuquihua.	mahn-kah-NAH-hah-YAH-poo ah-shoo-KEE-wah

Brazil

Brazilian cooking varies significantly from region to region. Unfortunately for the vegetarian visitor, most regional cuisine relies on meat, and in rural Amazonia you may even encounter tapir, sloth, or armadillo on your plate if you aren't careful. Pesco-vegetarians will find that fish is available along the coast and throughout much of the interior, and spicy seafood dishes are a specialty of Bahia state. There are a few vegetarian restaurants in big cities like Rio, São Paulo, and Brasilia, and restaurants in urban areas usually offer salads or pasta. Many ordinary restaurants are slowly beginning to add meat-less entrees to their menus.

Due to the large number of immigrants and their descendants in Brazil, the cities also have European, Middle Eastern, and Chinese restaurants. São Paolo has a large Japanese population, and Japanese dishes are easily available there; Japanese food (particularly sushi) is becoming trendy in other parts of the country as well. Brazil has plenty of good fruit and fruit juices, bread, and cheese, so an impromptu picnic is always a possibility. And for better or for worse, the usual complement of American-style fast-food restaurants can be found in most urban areas.

Outside (and to a certain extent, inside) the cities, vegetarianism is con-sidered terribly odd but acceptable; many poor Brazilians are *de facto* vegetarians living on beans and rice or manioc. Vegetarian travelers will have the greatest difficulties in southern Brazil, a land of friendly but militant red meat eaters. In this place of cowboys and *churrasco*—grilled beef—vegetarians are tolerated but certainly not catered to.

Brazilian **Portuguese** is the official language. Spanish (p. 26) is similar enough to Portuguese to be understood, although Spanish-speakers will not understand the responses. French (p. 66) is probably the most common second language, although English is spoken in tourist centers.

Portuguese

I would like something without _____.	Eu gostaria de algo sem _____.	eyoh gohs-tah-REE-ah jee AHL-goh saym _____.
We would like something without _____.	Nos gostariamos de algo sem _____.	nohs gohs-tah-ree-AH-mohs jee AHL-goh saym _____.
We would like something without _____. (colloquial version)	A gente quer alguma coisa que não tenha _____.	ah JEN-chee kehr ahl-GOO-mah KOY-zah kay now TAYN-yah _____.
I do not eat _____.	Eu não como _____.	eyoh now KOH-moh _____.
I eat _____ and _____.	Eu como _____ e _____.	eyoh KOH-moh ___ ee ___.
meat	carne	KAHR-nee
chicken	galinha	gah-LEEN-yah
fish	peixe	PAY-shay
eggs	ovos	AW-vohs
cheese	queijo	KAY-zhoo

I am a vegetarian. (male speaker)	Eu sou vegetariano.	eyoh soh vay-zhay-tah-ree-AH-noh
I am a vegetarian. (female speaker)	Eu sou vegetariana.	eyoh soh vay-zhay-tah-ree-AH-nah
Please	Por favor	pohr fah-VOHR
Thank you (male speaker)	Obrigado	oh-bree-GAH-doh
Thank you (female speaker)	Obrigada	oh-bree-GAH-dah

Chile

Unlike in neighboring Argentina, where meat is served separately in a large hunk, main dishes in Chile often consist of bits of meat mixed together with all the other ingredients in your meal. The same is true of most soup. Naturally, this presents a problem for vegetarian diners. There are vegetarian restaurants in Santiago and the regional capitals, and meatless pasta dishes or salads are usually available at restaurants in urban areas and tourist centers. Pizza is a common snack item. Assorted European and other international cuisines are well-represented in the larger cities and in touristed areas such as ski resorts or the central coast; these restaurants often offer at least one meatless entree.

In rural areas, people may regard vegetarians as deprived and think they are doing vegetarians a favor by giving them meat. With concerted effort, you should be able to have your way. Fish-eaters will have an easier time, as seafood is available everywhere and eel is the national dish.

Spanish (p. 26) is the national language. Some Aymará (p. 41) is spoken in the far northeast. A few scattered immigrant communities speak Italian or German.

Colombia

Although vegetarianism is considered very strange in most of the country, especially in the interior, it has become more acceptable in recent years and a few vegetarian restaurants have opened in the cities. European and Asian restaurants also exist in the cities, and one can usually find pasta, pizza, or some other viable meatless alternative. Colombia's cuisine is highly regional, but unfortunately the regions all use lots of meat; guinea pig is considered a delicacy in the southern interior. Rice and beans are usually available (but beware of lard), and yogurt is plentiful.

Spanish (p. 26) is the official language. A few communities in the Andes speak indigenous languages.

Ecuador
Vegetarianism is an oddity in Ecuador. However, in Quito and Cuenca it is fairly easy to find vegetarian restaurants, usually run by foreigners. General tourist-oriented restaurants, while usually not specifically vegetarian, commonly offer meatless dishes. Soy milk and tofu are available in cities. The cities also have a fair variety of Italian, Asian, or (heaven help us) North American–style restaurants. In smaller towns, restaurants will usually prepare meals without meat upon request. Yogurt is very popular throughout the country, and many soups are meatless, especially in the highlands. Bars often serve meatless side dishes; just be prepared for a few pointed questions if you don't drink beer.

Spanish (p. 26) is the official language. Many Indians speak indigenous languages; the most common of these is **Quechua** (p. 47).

French Guiana
Beans and rice or tubers served with meat or fish is the typical meal. However, bakeries, *creperies*, and French restaurants are also found throughout the country. There are also Vietnamese and East Indian restaurants that serve meatless dishes. French Guiana is home to cayenne pepper; unsurprisingly, Guianese food is often spicy.

French (p. 66) is the official language of French Guiana. Some Asian immigrant groups speak their native languages, and several Amerindian groups in the interior speak indigenous tongues.

Guyana
Guyana has many citizens of South Asian descent, and as a result vegetarianism is generally accepted and understood. The population is a polyglot of

races and cultures—African, Creole, Native American, Asian, Portuguese, and English—and the country's cuisine reflects this diversity. Unfortunately, most of these otherwise diverse dishes contain meat. Seafood, usually with rice, is very common. Curries and roti are often available in meatless form, and salted roast chickpeas are sold as a snack on the street. There are Chinese restaurants in the main towns. Most Guyanese pastries contain vegetable shortening instead of lard.

English is the official language. Most Guyanese speak a Creole dialect in addition to standard English. Amerindian languages, Hindi (p. 180), and other Asian languages are spoken in some areas.

Paraguay

Although Paraguayans seem to accept vegetarianism, it is far from common behavior. Meat is standard in the Paraguayan diet. Fortunately, many dishes contain only cheese. *Sopa Paraguayana*, a kind of soufflé, is often made without meat. Pasta, rice, and vegetables are usually available as side dishes in restaurants, and Asunción has European and American-style restaurants that occasionally serve acceptable meatless dishes.

The official languages are **Spanish** (p. 26) and **Guaraní**. Most Paraguayans are bilingual, but Guaraní is usually spoken by preference outside Asunción.

Guaraní

I do not eat ____.	Che ndakarúi ____.	sheh ndah-kah-ROO-ee ____.
I eat ____ and ____.	Che akaru ____ ha ____.	sheh ah-kah-ROO ____ hah ____.
meat	so'o	soh-oh
chicken	ryguasu	rih-wah-SOO
fish (also means "skin")	pire	peer-deh

eggs (literally, "hen's eggs")	ryguasu lupi'a	rih-wah-SOO loo-pee-UH
cheese	kesu	kay-SOO
Thank you	Aguije ndeve	ah-wee-JEH ndeh-veh

Peru

The national dish of Peru is *cuy*, or guinea pig (which fortunately is not often on the menu of tourist-oriented restaurants). Although vegetarianism is not widely practiced, those who do not want their dinner plucked from a Habitrail have a few options. Italian, Asian, and other world cuisines (as well as American fast-food restaurants, alas) are found in the cities, and there are even a few specialty vegetarian restaurants. Urban supermarkets stock tofu and soy milk. In tourist centers such as Lima and Cuzco, enterprising foreigners have opened vegetarian-friendly restaurants that cater mostly to North American and European travelers. Outside these areas, or if the expatriate scene is not your cup of coca tea, you can ask restaurants to prepare a special meatless meal. Potatoes in various forms are consumed everywhere. There are also many Chinese restaurants (known as *chifas*), even in fairly small towns.

Spanish (p. 26) is spoken in most of the country. Aymará (p. 41) is spoken in some parts of the Andes, as is **Quechua**. There are many local indigenous languages spoken in the eastern jungle. Over two million Amerindians in Peru speak no Spanish whatsoever.

Quechua

With over 30 dialects spread among 6–10 million speakers throughout the Andean countries, there is no such creature as "standard" Quechua. The few phrases listed below are from a common Peruvian dialect, and should be at least partly understood by most Quechua speakers.

I do not eat any kind of meat.	Mana ima laya aychata mikunichu.	MAH-nah EE-mah LAH-yah eye-CHAH-tah mee-koo-NEE-choo

Please	Allichu	ah-YEE-choo
Thank you	Yusulpayki	yoo-sool-PAY-kee

Suriname

Thanks to Suriname's large population of Indians and Indonesians, meatless dishes are available in most areas of the country. The vast majority of the population lives along the coast, and seafood, usually served with rice, is a staple.

Dutch (p. 61) is the official language, although a native dialect called Sranan Tonga is the everyday language of most Surinamese. Standard English is widely spoken. Hindi (p. 180) and Javanese (p. 213) are spoken among the Asian community.

Uruguay

Uruguayans tend to brag about the high quality of their beef, and their meat intake is nearly as high as that of their Argentine neighbors. However, cholesterol consciousness is taking hold and vegetarian food is not too difficult to find. Montevideo has several vegetarian restaurants and a surprising number of macrobiotic food stores, many of which sell prepared meals. The city also has a good variety of European-type restaurants which usually serve a meatless dish or two; the coastal resorts also have a good selection of restaurants. Even outside Montevideo, most restaurants offer at least one meatless entree (usually centered around pasta or salad).

Spanish (p. 26) is spoken throughout the country. Some localized immigrant groups speak other European languages.

Venezuela

In Caracas, vegetarianism has become fashionable in some quarters over the last few years (partly because of the high cost of beef), so it is fairly easy to go meatless. Zona Las Mercedes has a concentration of vegetarian restaurants, and there are many ethnic restaurants (Indian, Middle Eastern, Italian) throughout the city where it is possible to get meatless food. Outside Caracas, vegetarianism is much less common, and many rural people consider it an extremely strange custom that leads to thin blood and weakness. Even apparently meatless dishes often contain bits of bacon or pork. The best option in rural areas is probably to create meals from side orders, and to make your dietary desires clear.

Spanish (p. 26) is the official language.

Europe

To many people whose forebears emigrated from Europe, the food of that continent is the most immediately familiar type of foreign cuisine, and various common dishes of European origin are well-known throughout much of the world. Of course, there is no such thing as "typical" European food; depending on his or her ethnic background and a host of other factors, a person thinking of European food might envision anything from pasta and pizza to fish and chips to borscht to escargot.

Although much European food appears immediately familiar to a visitor, Europe is a polyglot of cultures and of cuisines, and almost every country in Europe offers a variety of regional and local dishes that will be utterly unfamiliar. Some of these dishes will be vegetarian, some may be vegan, and others will contain meat or meat stock. (Still others may be vaguely frightening regardless of their meat content.) It is therefore impossible to generalize with any degree of usefulness about the availability of meatless food—except to say that vegetarianism is most common in northern Europe, least accepted in eastern Europe, and generally easier to practice in cities than in rural areas. With perseverance, you should be able to find something meatless to keep you alive anywhere, and with luck that something will actually be nutritious and tasty.

This chapter is divided, based on loose linguistic, cultural, and geographic affinities among countries, into three sections: Northern Europe, Southern Europe, and Eastern Europe.

A. NORTHERN EUROPE

The cuisines of northern European countries traditionally centered on the consumption of meat or fish. These carnivorous habits resulted partly from geography and climate and partly from the relative affluence of these countries. Especially during the last 20 years, this affluence, combined with increasing health consciousness and ecological sensibility, has resulted in a growing concentration of vegetarians in this part of the world. There are substantial numbers of vegetarians (and vegetarian organizations) here, and the upshot is that northern Europe is on the whole one of the easiest places in the world for vegetarian travel. In most (but not all) northern countries, it is reasonably easy to find specialty vegetarian, vegan, or whole-food restaurants, or meatless meals on the menus of ordinary restaurants. As elsewhere in the developed world, however, the range of vegetarian options is better in large towns and cities than in rural areas.

Austria
While Austrian food is traditionally very heavy and meat-oriented (think of *wiener schnitzel*), the situation for vegetarians is improving. Most larger Austrian towns have one or two vegetarian restaurants; Vienna has several, including some exclusively vegan establishments. In cities and resort areas, many ordinary restaurants offer at least one vegetarian entree. There are also a fair number of ethnic restaurants (particularly Indian, Middle Eastern, and Asian) that serve vegetarian meals. Non-vegans can subsist if necessary on Austrian dairy products, which are uniformly excellent.

German (p. 56) is the principal language in Austria. English is a common second language.

Belgium
Classic Belgian cuisine is widely acclaimed. Vegetarians might not feel so enthusiastic, because Belgians tend to use lots of meat. (Belgian chocolate, thankfully, tends to be meat-free.) Most larger towns have at least one vegetarian restaurant, and Brussels has a wide variety of vegetarian restaurants. Ordinary Belgian restaurants are beginning to offer meatless entrees, or at least entree-sized salads. There are also plenty of Asian restaurants and

Middle Eastern fast-food establishments, almost all of which serve some vegetarian food. While they are unlikely to provide the staple of your diet, waffle stands can be found everywhere.

Flemish and **French** (p. 66) are the national languages. Generally, French is spoken in the south of the country, while Flemish is spoken in the north. Brussels is officially bilingual. Although there are some minor differences in dialect, Flemish is essentially the same language as **Dutch** (p. 61).

Denmark

Vegetarianism is quite common in Denmark, and just about every restaurant in Copenhagen and other cities and large towns has one or more meatless dishes on the menu. There are also some veggie-friendly ethnic restaurants, as well as a number of exclusively vegetarian or vegan restaurants. In the smaller towns of Jutland (on the mainland), it is sometimes difficult to obtain vegetarian entrees; occasionally you may be forced to make do with potatoes and boiled vegetables. If you can find a good traditional breakfast, which usually features cereal, fruit, and cheese (as well as meat and fish), you might be sated until dinner. Most fast food in Denmark is meat-based, but the common *smørrebrød*—traditional open-faced sandwiches—are sometimes made with cheese or vegetables.

Danish is the national language. English is widely spoken as a second language.

Danish

I would like something without ____.	Jeg vil gerne have noget uden ___.	yai vihll GAIR-nuhr HAY noh-weht OO-then ____.
We would like something without ____.	Vi vil gerne have noget uden ____.	vee vihll GAIR-nuhr HAY noh-weht OO-then ____.
I do not eat ____.	Jeg spiser ikke ___.	yai SPEE-zuhr ICK-kuh ___.

I eat _____ and _____.	Jeg spiser ___ og ___.	yai SPEE-zuhr ___ oh ___.
meat	kød	koo-uhd
chicken	kylling	kyoo-ling
fish	fisk	fihsk
eggs	æg	ehg
cheese	ost	oost
I am a vegetarian.	Jeg er vegetar.	yai air VEEG-eh-tahr
Thank you	Tak	tahkk

The largely self-governing **Faeroe Islands**, awash in the frigid North Atlantic, are not exactly a haven for vegetarians. The main foods are fish, dried mutton or other meat (occasionally including beached whale) served with potatoes; fresh vegetables are scarce. The people speak Faeroese, an ancient Scandinavian tongue that is similar to Icelandic (p. 58). Danish is usually spoken as a second language.

Greenland (Kalaallit Nunaat), despite the promising name, is one of the least congenial spots on earth for non-pesco vegetarians. (Fish eaters should be fine.) Most green growing things must be imported, and are extraordinarily expensive even when available. Most Greenlanders learn Danish in school; their native language, Greenlandic, is an Inuit (Eskimo) tongue.

Finland

Vegetarianism is not unheard of in Finland, but is not as common as in Denmark or Sweden. In Finnish cities, one can usually find at least one meatless entree on most menus. There are several vegetarian and many veggie-friendly restaurants in Helsinki. Fish eaters will be happy anywhere, but outside the cities strict vegetarian options are thin on the ground. Beware of well-intentioned Finns encouraging you to eat the local game, such as Donner,

Blitzen, and all the other reindeer. If you can find them, there are some good traditional meatless soups, particularly cold fruit soup. A last (or first) resort might be one of the pizzerias that are found in towns throughout Finland.

Finnish is the national language. Swedish is also widely spoken, especially in the west. English is a common second language in and near the larger cities.

Finnish

I would like something without ____.	Haluaisin jotakin ilman ____.	HAH-loo-eye-sihn YAW-tah-kihn EEL-mahn ____.
We would like something without ____.	Haluaisimme jotakin ilman ____.	HAH-loo-eye-sihm-meh YAW-tah-kihn EEL-mahn ____.
I do not eat ____.	En syö ____.	ehn syoo ____.
I eat ____ and ____.	Syön ____ ja ____.	SYOO-ehn ____ yah ____.
meat	lihaa	LIH-hah
chicken	kanaa	KAH-nah
fish	kalaa	KAH-lah
eggs	munaa	MOO-nah
cheese	juusto	YOOS-taw
I am a vegetarian.	Olen kasvissyöjä.	AW-lehn KAHSS-viss-yoo-yah
Thank you	Kiitos	KEE-tawss

Germany

Although traditional German cooking is heavy on red meat, particularly pork and what might be euphemistically called pork products, Germany is by no means the *wurst* country in the world for vegetarians. In western Germany, vegetarianism is very common and there are significant numbers of vegans. Most cities and large towns have vegetarian or natural food restaurants, and many mainstream restaurants offer one or more meatless entrees. At the very least, you should be able to get salad and pasta or pizza. There are also many ethnic restaurants, especially Middle Eastern and Indian, serving up vegetarian fare. For picnics or self-made snacks, German bread and cheese are cheap, tasty, and filling.

In formerly Communist eastern Germany (apart from Berlin), vegetarianism has not yet established itself and it may be difficult to avoid meat. While the concept of vegetarianism is creeping eastward, many restaurants still serve only meat or fish entrees. A few vegetarian restaurants have opened in the cities, but creativity may be called for elsewhere. For the next few years, standard German side dishes such as sauerkraut and assorted potato concoctions may have to suffice.

German, with regional differences in dialect and pronunciation, is spoken throughout the country. English is a common second language, especially in the west.

German

I would like something without ____.	Ich hätte gerne etwas ohne ____.	**ikh** HEH-teh GAIR-neh EHT-vahss OH-neh ____.
We would like something without ____.	Wir hätten gerne etwas ohne ____.	veer HEH-tehn GAIR-neh EHT-vahss OH-neh ____.
I do not eat ____.	Ich esse kein ____.	**ikh** EH-seh kyne ____.
I eat ____ and ____.	Ich esse ____ und ____.	**ikh** EH-seh ____ oont ____.

meat	fleisch	flysh
chicken	huhn	hoon
fish	fisch	fish
eggs	eier	EYE-uhr
cheese	käse	KAY-zeh
I am a vegetarian. (female speaker)	Ich bin vegetarierin.	**ikh** bihn feh-geh-TAH-ree-ehr-een
I am a vegetarian. (male speaker)	Ich bin vegetarier.	**ikh** binn feh-geh-TAH-reer
Please	Bitte	BIH-tuh
Thank you	Danke	DAHN-kuh

Great Britain

Great Britain is the home of such vegetarian nightmares as roast beef, steak and kidney pie, and haggis. Britain also happens to be the home of one of the largest groups of vegetarians in Europe. This situation is somewhat ironic, considering that meat is one of the few things the British historically have been able to cook well. Fortunately, the overall quality and variety of British restaurants has improved significantly in recent years. There are vegetarian or wholefood restaurants in most large and many small towns throughout Britain. The majority of restaurants and a large number of pubs now offer vegetarian entrees. There are even a few vegetarian resorts and bed and breakfast hotels scattered around the country. As an extra safeguard for worried vegetarians, Britain's status as former imperial and merchant power means that restaurants representing cuisines from all corners of the world exist in Britain. Indian restaurants and take-aways are particularly common, even in fairly small towns.

Despite the relative ease of vegetarian travel in Britain, all is not well in the homeland of mad cow disease. British fast food, like American fast food, is heavily meat-oriented. In very small towns, especially in rural Wales, Scotland, Northern Ireland, and the north of England, it may be difficult to get a decent meal without meat. Lard is still commonly used for frying. And even in the cities, some restaurants do not serve meatless entrees (although even some steakhouses have vegetarian plates). All things considered, however, it is relatively easy for a vegetarian to keep well fed in Britain.

It should surprise no one that **English** is the main language of Great Britain. While the accent in some regions may *sound* like a foreign language, English-speaking visitors should have few problems being understood. A few people in the far west and north speak Welsh or Scottish Gaelic as a first language.

Iceland

Unlike its mainland Scandinavian cousins, Iceland is not a very nice land for vegetarians. There is at least one vegetarian restaurant in Reykjavík, but the situation is otherwise fairly bleak. Icelanders eat what they can produce on or around their none-too-fertile island—in other words, fish, sheep, and poultry or sea birds. Imported food is extravagantly expensive. People who resolutely refuse to eat fish will probably be driven to cooking for themselves or living off side dishes at restaurants. Vegans may slowly waste away. As some compensation, Icelandic bread is good and cheese and yogurt are widespread and tasty.

The national language is **Icelandic**, an archaic descendant of Old Norse. Many Icelanders speak excellent English.

Icelandic

I would like something without ____.	Gæti ég fengið eitthvað ekki með ____.	gye-tih yehgg fehn-gith ayte-vahth ehk-kee mehth ____.
We would like something without ____.	Gætum við fengið eitthvað ekki með ____.	gye-turm vith fehn-gith ayte-vahth ehk-kee mehth ____.
meat	kjöti	KYUHR-tay

chicken	kjúklingi	kyook-leen-gay
fish	fiski	fihss-kee
eggs	eggjum	ehg-yurm
cheese	osti	ohss-tee
I do not eat _____.	Ég borða ekki _____.	yehg BOHR-thaw ehk-kee _____.
I eat _____ **and** _____.	Ég borða _____ og _____.	yehg BOHR-thaw _____ ohrg _____.
meat	kjöt	kyuhrt
chicken	kjúkling	kyook-lihng
fish	fisk	fihsk
eggs	egg	ehg
cheese	ost	ohsst
I am a vegetarian.	Ég er grænmetisæta.	yehg ehr gryne-meh-tihss-EYE-tah
Thank you	Takk	tahk

Ireland

It is said that a person stranded on a desert island could survive on Guinness alone. Presumably most people would desire additional sustenance, and while Ireland may be many things, it is not a culinary paradise for vegetarians. It is certainly possible to get meatless meals in Ireland: There are some vegetarian restaurants, although these are relatively few and far between, and an increasing number of mainstream restaurants are beginning to add meatless entrees to their menus. There are also various ethnic restaurants, particularly in Dublin, as well as the standard collection of pizza and pasta places.

Off the beaten path, however, it remains difficult to avoid lamb (which may appear in any number of guises, especially Irish stew). Fish eaters will have little problem, even in the countryside, but others may have to survive on carbohydrates alone: Potatoes are abundant (the famine having ended a century and a half ago), and Irish breads are some of the most unique and delicious in the world. Seaweed is harvested and eaten as a regular food.

English is spoken almost everywhere. A few communities, mainly on the west coast, speak Irish Gaelic as a first language, but almost everyone understands English.

Luxembourg

Luxembourg is so small that it cannot really be said to have a distinctive cuisine of its own. The food generally features lots of meat and resembles traditional German or Belgian cooking. A good percentage of restaurants serve vegetarian dishes such as pasta or salads, but one cannot expect great variety and creativity in Luxembourgish meatless offerings.

French (p. 66), **German** (p. 56), and Letzeburgesch (a Germanic dialect) are the official languages. English and other European languages are spoken by many residents, especially in the capital.

Netherlands

Although traditional Dutch cuisine is meat-and-potatoes oriented, the Netherlands is nonetheless one of the easiest European countries in which to be vegetarian. There are many specialized vegetarian restaurants in the cities and towns, and most general restaurants have at least one or two vegetarian options on the menu; sometimes they offer a rather extensive selection. The cities, particularly Amsterdam and Rotterdam, have an impressive array of often meatless ethnic food on offer; Indonesian, Surinamese, and Middle Eastern food is the most common. Non-vegans are in for quite a good time in the Netherlands—anyone who loves cheese and does not find happiness in Holland may wish to seek professional help. Dutch bread is also excellent, and whole-grain varieties are commonplace. However, Dutch snacks and fast food still tend to focus on meat. In addition, meatless dishes may be harder to find (although they do exist) in small towns, especially in the south and east.

Dutch is the official language. Many people in the Netherlands speak

English almost as well as (or better than) you, and may cringe at your attempts to speak their difficult native language.

Dutch

I would like something without _____.	Ik vil graag iets zonder _____.	ihk fihl **khrahkh** eets SOHN-duhr _____.
We would like something without _____.	Wij villen graag iets zonder _____.	vay FIHL-lehn **khrahkh** eets SOHN-duhr _____.
I do not eat _____.	Ik eet geen _____.	ihk ayte **khayn** _____.
I eat _____ and _____.	Ik eet _____ en _____.	ihk ayte _____ ehn _____.
meat	vlees	flayss
chicken	kip	kihp
fish	vis	fihss
eggs	eieren	EYE-yuh-rehn
cheese	kaas	kahs
I am a vegetarian.	Ik ben vegetariër.	ihk behn FEH-**kh**uh-TAH-ree-uhr
Please (to elders and others you wish to address respectfully)	Alstublieft	ahls-TOO-bleeft
Please (to people in the same social class)	Alsjeblieft	ahls-YUH-bleeft

Thank you (respectful)	Dank u wel	dahn koo vehl
Thank you (to people in the same social class)	Dankje wel	dahn-KYUH vehl

Norway

It is not an easy or enviable task to be a vegetarian in Norway, but the concept is gradually becoming more acceptable, especially among younger people. Oslo has several vegetarian restaurants, and the city's ordinary restaurants are slowly incorporating meatless dishes into their menus. Outside Oslo, however, it remains difficult to find good vegetarian meals; along the northern coastline, it is almost impossible. Since Norwegians have traditionally eaten fish virtually by the boatload, pesco-vegetarians are in an excellent position. Lacto-vegetarians may be able to subsist on Jarlsberg or other Norwegian cheeses. Vegans are likely to be utterly miserable. Some traditional soups do not contain meat or fish (although they are often prepared with meat stock). Most towns have pizza places, and an occasional Middle Eastern or Chinese restaurant can be found. A good strategy might be to fill up at breakfast, which is usually a buffet featuring cheese, bread, yogurt and fruit (as well as fish and meat).

Norwegian is the national language. Most Norwegians can speak at least minimal English, although they appreciate attempts to speak their language.

Norwegian

I would like something without _____.	Jeg vil gjerne ha noe uten _____.	yay veel YEHR-nuh hah noo-weh EW-tehn _____.
We would like something without _____.	Vi vil gjerne ha noe uten _____.	vee veel YEHR-nuh hah noo-weh EW-tuhn _____.
I do not eat _____.	Jeg spiser ikke _____.	yay SPEE-suhr EEK-kuh _____.

I eat ____ and ____.	Jeg spiser ____ og ____.	yay SPEE-suhr ____ oah ____.
meat	kjøtt	hyuht
chicken	kylling	SHEW-ling
fish	fisk	feesk
eggs	egg	ehg
cheese	ost	oost
I am a vegetarian.	Jeg er vegetarianer.	yayg ahr veh-geh-tah-ree-AH-nuhr
Thank you	Takk	tahk

Sweden

Although the traditional Swedish diet is heavy on fish (or meat) and potatoes, there are many vegetarians and vegans in Sweden. Stockholm proudly offers several specialist vegetarian restaurants, and most Swedish cities have at least one. Many ordinary restaurants offer at least one or two meatless dishes. In addition, there is a slew of pizzerias and Chinese, Middle Eastern, and Indian restaurants in the cities. One need not go ethnic, however; it is easy to fill up on buffets at breakfast (bread, cereal, jams, eggs, spreads, yogurt) and *smörgåsbords* at lunch (cheese, eggs, salads, and potatoes, in addition to unwelcome herring and cold cuts). Swedes also make interesting traditional soups, such as fruit soup, although these are hard to find in restaurants.

Although Sweden is a decent country for the vegetarian traveler, it can occasionally be difficult to find something meatless to munch in rural areas and the far north. Herring is omnipresent, so fish-eaters will never lack something to eat. Salads are served in most places, and Swedish dairy products such as yogurt are available everywhere. Sweden produces interesting and unique berries, such as the Arctic cloudberry (which is available out of season in preserves).

Swedish is the national language. English is spoken by a majority of the population as a second language.

Swedish

I would like something without _____.	Jag skulle önska någonting utan _____.	yahg skew-luh URN-skuh NOH-goon-teeng EW-tahn _____.
We would like something without _____.	Vi skulle önska någonting utan _____.	vee skew-luh URN-skuh NOH-goon-teeng EW-tahn _____.
I do not eat _____.	Jag äter inte _____.	yahg EH-tehr IHN-teh _____.
I eat _____ and _____.	Jag äter _____ och _____.	yahg EH-tehr _____ awk _____.
meat	kött	shuhrt
chicken	höna	HUHR-nuh
fish	fisk	fihsk
eggs	ägg	ehg
cheese	ost	oost
I am a vegetarian.	Jag är vegitarian.	yahg ehr veh-geh-tah-ree-AHN
Thank you	Tack	tuhk

Switzerland

Traditional Swiss food is heavy and filling, as befits the cuisine of a mountain people. Meat is the favorite centerpiece of a meal, but the Swiss also make many potato dishes, such as *rösti* (a potato pancake), that are filling enough to constitute a main course. Both pasta and pizza are common dishes in restaurants, and more creative meatless dishes are becoming more available. A few exclusively vegetarian restaurants have begun to open in Swiss cities. Outside the cities, the abundance of renowned Swiss cheese will keep non-vegan stomachs happy and cholesterol levels high; Switzerland is home to fondue and other cheese dishes such as *raclette*. If ponderous Swiss food becomes wearisome, cities and resort areas have restaurants and fast-food stands serving more international offerings, such as Middle Eastern, Greek, or Indian food.

Switzerland has three official languages. In the west of the country, **French** (p. 66) is the principal language. **Italian** (p. 70) is spoken in parts of the south. A very few people speak a Romance language called Romansch, while the majority of Swiss speak various **German** (p. 56) dialects, some of which are nearly impossible for outsiders to understand. (Instead of using coded transmissions, the Swiss army sometimes uses soldiers from remote mountain areas as radio operators.) Most people who are unfortunate enough to have to deal regularly with tourists can speak English.

The food of tiny **Liechtenstein** is virtually indistinguishable from that of Switzerland. The language is a dialect of German.

B. SOUTHERN EUROPE

Southern Europe presents something of a paradox to the discerning vegetarian. On one hand, traditional southern European cooking in general relies less on meat as a central ingredient than other European cuisines do. On the other hand, intentional vegetarianism is still an object of befuddlement to many people in this part of the world. Therefore, while it is usually not overly difficult to find something meatless to eat, there is a relative scarcity of specialty vegetarian restaurants. In some cases, it may take some searching to find wholly vegetarian entrees, free of meat stock and devoid of random bits of meat or fish. Pesco-vegetarians should have no difficulty anywhere within areas near the Mediterranean Sea, and strict vegetarians always have the solace of a beautiful climate and abundant fruits and vegetables.

France
French cooking combines aspects of both the northern European meat fixation and the lighter tradition of Mediterranean cooking. The result is a cuisine that is highly regarded and highly regional. One problem is that the

French industriously use almost every edible portion of an animal, and process it into a variety of sometimes innocuous-seeming items; eating unfamiliar food here is the gastronomic equivalent of navigating a mine field.

Generally, people in northern France consume more meat; however, intentional vegetarianism is more commonly practiced in the north, and most cities and large towns have vegetarian or health food restaurants. Fortunately, many entrees in ordinary French restaurants are free of meat, fish, and mystery organs, and of course bakeries and *patisseries* always offer enticing carbohydrates. In the south of France, fish is an important part of the diet. Meals become lighter in the south, fresh vegetables and fruits are more prevalent, and the influence of nearby Italy creeps in in the form of pasta dishes. There are relatively few vegetarian restaurants, but the wider use of green growing things in everyday cooking makes this scarcity less of an obstacle.

While it seems almost criminal to come to France and avoid French cooking entirely, in the towns and cities a variety of foreign cuisines are available as either a consistent alternative or a temporary change of pace. North African, Middle Eastern, and southeast Asian restaurants are the most common due to French colonization patterns, but many other cuisines are represented. And it is perfectly possible (and by no means unpleasant) to live off French bread, cheese, fruit, yogurt and of course wine—all of which are available even in the most remote villages whose inhabitants would sooner eat a duck whole than throw it bread.

French is the official language. Some visitors to Paris may find themselves the subject of ridicule either for not speaking French or for speaking it improperly. The situation is considerably more relaxed outside the capital, and most attempts to speak the language will be welcomed. Basque (p. 77) is spoken in a few areas in the far southwest, some Italian (p. 70) and Catalan (p. 76) is spoken in the south and southeast, and German is common in Alsace-Lorraine. Arabic (p. 110) is spoken by many immigrants from North Africa.

French

I would like something without ____.	Je voudrais manger quelque chose sans ____.	zhuh voo-dray mahn-zhay kelk shohs sah**n** ____.

We would like something without ____.	Nous voudrions manger qualque chose sans ____.	noo voo-dree-ohn mahn-zhay kelk shohs sahn ____.
meat	viande	vee-ohnd
chicken	poulet	poo-lay
fish	poisson	pwahs-sawn
eggs	ouefs	zuhrf
cheese	fromage	froh-mahzh
I do not eat ____.	Je ne mange pas ____.	zhuh nuh mahnzh pah ____.
meat	de viande	duh vee-ohnd
chicken	de poulet	duh poo-lay
fish	de poisson	duh pwahs-sawn
eggs	d'ouefs	duhrf
cheese	de fromage	duh froh-mahzh
I eat ____ and ____.	Je mange ____ et ____.	zhuh mahnzh ____ ay ____.
meat	la viande	lah vee-ohnd
chicken	le poulet	luh poo-lay
fish	le poisson	luh pwahs-sawn
eggs	les ouefs	lay zuhrf
cheese	le fromage	luh froh-mahzh

I am a vegetarian. (male speaker)	Je suis végétarien.	zhuh swee vay-zhay-tah-ree-yeh**n**
I am a vegetarian. (female speaker)	Je suis végétarienne.	zhuh swee vay-zhay-tah-ree-yeh**nn**
Please	Si'l vous plaît	seel voo play
Thank you	Merci	MAYR-see

The food of **Monaco**, insofar as it can be said to have its own cuisine at all, is very much like that of southern France. French is the official language.

Greece

While meaty *souvlaki* and *gyros* are the most familiar representatives of Greek cuisine, vegetarian travelers have a variety of meatless dishes at their disposal. These dishes typically contain rice, eggplant (aubergine), or assorted vegetables, but they may not always be available at restaurants targeted at tourists. Fish-eaters will have no problem; along the coast and on the islands (in other words, in most of Greece), fish or shellfish is the usual main course. Unfortunately for strict vegetarians, menu variety may consist of having several species of fish from which to choose, rather than offering anything that could be classified as "non-fish." Even in such fishy circumstances, snacks such as cheese pies and *spanakopita* (spinach turnovers), are ubiquitous, and Greek salad is served at almost every restaurant. Greek *tavernas* provide an excellent option; these usually serve a wide variety of appetizers, many of which do not have meat and which can be put together to make a substantial meal. Pizza and pasta are also common menu items at restaurants.

Greek is the national language of Greece. Note that the Greek word for vegetarian literally means "vegetable-eater," and is sometimes used as a synonym for crazy. Be careful not to use the word out of context! The following phrases have been transliterated from the Greek alphabet.

Greek

I would like something without _____.	Tha íthela káti horís _____.	thah EE-theh-lah KAH-tee **kh**oh-REESE _____.
We would like something without _____.	Tha thélame káti horís _____.	thah THEH-lah-meh KAH-tee **kh**oh-REESE _____.
I do not eat _____.	Dhén tróyo _____.	thehnn TROH-yoh _____.
I eat _____ and _____.	Tróyo _____ ke _____.	TROH-yoh _____ keh _____.
meat	kréas	KREH-ahss
chicken	kotópoulo	koh-TOH-poo-loh
fish	psári	PSAH-ree
eggs	avgó	ahv-GHOH
cheese	tirí	tee-REE
I am a vegetarian. (male speaker)	Íme hortophágos.	EE-meh hohr-toh-FAH-**kh**ohss
I am a vegetarian. (female speaker)	Íme hortophága.	EE-meh hohr-toh-FAH-**kh**ah
Please	Parakaló	pah-rah-kah-LOH
Thank you	Efkaristó	ehf-**kh**ah-ree-STOH

Italy

Volumes have been written on Italian cuisine, so there is no need for this book to launch into an in-depth analysis of the differences between the sublime cuisine of Tuscany and the delightful cuisine of Lombardy. It is sufficient to note that cooking in Italy varies dramatically from region to region, but the one constant—and friend to vegetarians throughout the world—is pasta. While both the form of the pasta and the accompanying ingredients change, it should usually be possible to find some meatless, pasta-based dish almost anywhere in Italy. Salad is favored everywhere, and Italian breads and cheeses are legendary. Vegans may have trouble, although pasta with tomato sauce and no cheese is common. Some pizzas are made without cheese, especially in southern Italy where often only vegetable toppings are used. There are also many meatless side dishes and *antipasti*, and vegetable soups such as minestrone are very common. However, soups are sometimes made with chicken or meat stock, as are other apparently innocuous dishes such as risotto.

Although there are many meatless Italian dishes, vegetarianism as a deliberate practice is not always understood in Italy. In the cities, especially in the north, there are a few specialty vegetarian restaurants. However, more meat is consumed in the north, and veal, lamb, and chicken dishes are particularly prevalent; in a some cases, a restaurant may offer no meatless dishes at all. In the south, as well as in seaside resorts throughout the country, fish is more prominent. A North African influence becomes evident in Sicily and the far south, where rice, couscous, and lentil soup are common.

Italian is the national language. Although there are many regional dialects, the "standard" Italian given below should be understood everywhere.

Italian

English	Italian	Pronunciation
I would like something without _____.	Vorrei qualcosa senza _____.	vohr-RAYee kwahl-KOH-sah SAYN-tsah _____.
We would like something without _____.	Vorremmo qualcosa senza _____.	vohr-RAY-moh kwahl-KOH-sah SAYN-tsah _____.

I do not eat _____.	Non mangio _____.	nohn MAHN-joh _____.
I eat _____ and _____.	Mangio _____ e _____.	MAHN-joh _____ ay _____.
meat	carne	KAHR-nay
chicken	pollo	POH-loh
fish	pesce	PAY-shay
eggs	uova	oo-OH-vah
cheese	formaggio	fohr-MAHD-joh
I am a vegetarian. (female speaker)	Sono vegetariana.	SOH-noh vay-jay-tah-ree-AH-nah
I am a vegetarian. (male speaker)	Sono vegetariano.	SOH-noh vay-jay-tah-ree-AH-noh
Please	Per favore	pehr fah-VOH-ray
Thank you	Grazie	GRAH-tsee-eh

San Marino and **Vatican City** are tiny, nominally independent countries wholly surrounded by Italy. Vatican City is only one square mile, so apart from the Vatican snack shops the only food you are likely to encounter will be spiritual. The food in San Marino is basically that of northern Italy. **Italian** is the language of both countries. Due to the global influence of the Catholic Church, many other languages are spoken by the few residents of Vatican City.

Malta

Although Malta is a tiny cluster of islands, it has a unique cuisine of its own that blends Arab, Turkish, and Italian influences. Traditional Maltese cooking tends to include game such as rabbit and lamb, as well as plenty of fish. But surprisingly many options for vegetarians exist. Pasta such as spaghetti and traditional Maltese *ravjul* (ravioli) is available everywhere. There are many vegetable and bean soups, and a host of tangy sheep and goat cheeses. Bread with olive oil is served at every meal and sometimes as a snack, and most local or international-style restaurants serve an array of salads and vegetable appetizers. Unfortunately, the majority of restaurants cater to tourists, and mainly serve French and Italian entrees rather than more interesting local cuisine. A common offering of street vendors and bars is *pastizzi*, a pastry filled with cheese or vegetables (but occasionally with meat or fish).

The official languages are **English** and **Maltese**. Although most Maltese are proficient in English, it may be useful to be able to say a few words of Maltese, especially on the outer islands.

Maltese

I do not eat _____.	Ma niekolx ____.	mah nih-KOHLSH ____.
meat	laħam	LAH-hahm
chicken	ħut	hoot
fish	tiġieġ	TEE-jeech
eggs	bajd	byte
cheese	ġobon	JOH-bohn
I am a vegetarian. (female speaker)	Jiena veġetarjana.	yeh-nah veh-jeh-tahr-YAH-nah
I am a vegetarian. (male speaker)	Jiena veġetarjan.	yeh-nah veh-jeh-TAHR-yahn
Thank you	Grazzi	GRAH-tsee

Portugal

Portugal is one of the least vegetarian-friendly countries of southern Europe. The standard Portuguese diet is heavy on chicken, pork, and seafood—especially seafood. While pesco-vegetarians will be delighted at their prospects, strict vegetarians may have a difficult time in Portugal. There are a few vegetarian or vegetarian-friendly restaurants in Lisbon, Oporto, and in the resorts of the Algarve on the south coast. The cities also have a selection of restaurants serving other European, Middle Eastern, or Asian cuisines. Apart from these limited options, vegetarians may be restricted to salads, bread, cheese (or cheese sandwiches), fruit, and assorted vegetable side dishes. There are also plenty of vegetable soups on offer, although they often are based on stock or may even contain bits of meat "for flavor."

The national language is **Portuguese**. Although Portuguese as spoken in Brazil is perfectly intelligible to someone from Portugal, there are some differences in pronunciation. Therefore, Portuguese as spoken in Portugal is presented here separately.

Portuguese

I would like something without _____.	Eu gostaria de algo sem _____.	eyoo gohsh-tah-REE-ah duh AHL-goo saym _____.
We would like something without _____.	Nos gostariamos de algo sem _____.	noosh goosh-tah-ree-AH-mohs duh AHL-goo saym _____.
I do not eat _____.	Eu não como _____.	eyoo now KOH-moo _____.
I eat _____ and _____.	Eu como _____ e _____.	eyoo KOH-moo _____ ee _____.
meat	carne	KAHR-nuh
chicken	frango	FRAYN-goo
fish	peixe	PAY-shuh

eggs	ovos	AW-voos
cheese	queijo	KAY-zhoo
I am a vegetarian. (female speaker)	Eu sou vegetariana.	eyoo soh vay-zhay-tah-ree-AH-nah
I am a vegetarian. (male speaker)	Eu sou vegetariano.	eyoo soh vay-zhay-tah-ree-AH-noo
Please	Faz favor	fahsh fah-VOHR
Thank you (male speaker)	Obrigado	aw-bree-GAH-doo
Thank you (female speaker)	Obrigada	aw-bree-GAH-dah

Spain

Spanish cuisine is highly regional, but vegetarian entrees are not particularly common anywhere in Spain. In Barcelona, and to a lesser extent in Madrid and other large cities, there are some specialty vegetarian restaurants. Restaurants that are used to northern European tourists, especially more upscale establishments in cities and resort areas, are likely to offer at least one vegetarian entree. There are also Middle Eastern and North African restaurants in most large towns, and these usually serve some meatless dishes.

Choices elsewhere are slim. In Andalucia and along the coasts, fish is the most common meal centerpiece. Elsewhere, chicken, pork, or beef are usual. There are often meatless side dishes, but the range on offer will vary depending on region. Rice is reasonably common throughout the country, especially in the south where Arabic influence is greatest. Pizza, salads, or the Spanish *tortilla* (a potato omelette) are all typical offerings. And almost every bar, restaurant, or snack shop offers cheese sandwiches.

The best informal option for vegetarians probably is to indulge in *tapas*, assorted inexpensive appetizers, which are available in most bars in the evening. Many *tapas* are meatless or vegan, and are often far more interesting than main dishes served in nearby restaurants. *Tapas* can make a substantial meal if enough of them are eaten together.

The national language of Spain is Castillian **Spanish**. Most people in the country can understand the Castillian dialect, although Andalucian usage is more like that of Latin American Spanish (p. 26). There are also several distinct regional languages. **Catalan** is spoken in Barcelona and the rest of Catalonia, as well as in Valencia and on the Balearic Islands. **Basque**, which is unrelated to any other European language, is spoken in the Basque country of the western Pyrenees and along much of the coast of the Bay of Biscay. Other languages such as Galician and Murcian are also spoken in parts of northwest Spain.

Spanish

I would like something without _____.	Quisiera comer algo sin _____.	kee-see-YAIR-uh koh-MAIR AHL-goh seen _____.
We would like something without _____.	Quisieramos comer algo sin _____.	kee-see-YAIR-ah-mohs koh-MAIR AHL-goh seen _____.
I do not eat _____.	No como _____.	noh KOH-moh _____.
I eat _____ and _____.	Como _____ y _____.	KOH-moh _____ ee _____.
meat	carne	KAHR-nay
chicken	pollo	POHL-yoh
fish	pescado	peh-SKAH-doh
eggs	huevos	WAY-bohs
cheese	queso	KAY-soh
I am a vegetarian. (female speaker)	Soy vegetariana.	soy beh-heh-tah-ree-AH-nah

I am a vegetarian. (male speaker)	Soy vegetariano.	soy beh-heh-tah-ree-AH-noh
Please	Por favor	pohr fah-BOHR
Thank you	Gracias	GRAH-thee-ahs

Catalan

Catalan is divided into various dialects. The phrases below should be generally understood, although local usage may be different.

I do not eat _____.	No menjo _____.	noh MEHN-zhoo _____.
I eat _____ and _____.	Menjo _____ i _____.	MEHN-zhoo _____ ee _____.
meat	carn	kahrn
chicken	pollastre	puhl-YAH-struh
fish	peix	pehsh
eggs	ous	AW-oos
cheese	formatge	foor-MAHT-zhuh
I am a vegetarian. (male speaker)	Soc vegetariá.	sohk buh-zhuh-tuh-ree-AH
I am a vegetarian. (female speaker)	Soc vegetariana.	sohk buh-zhuh-tuh-ree-AH-nuh
Please	Si us plau	see oos plow
Thank you	Merces	muhr-SEHS
or	Gracies	GRAH-see-uhs

Basque

Basque usage and pronunciation vary from region to region. The phrases below should be understood by most Basque-speaking people, however.

I do not eat ____.	Nik ez dut ____ jaten.	nihk ehs doot ____ YAH-tehn.
	or	nihk ehs doot ____ HAH-tehn.
meat	okelarik	oh-KEH-lah-reek
chicken	ollokirik	oh-LOK-kih-reek
fish	arralnik	ahr-RAHL-neek
eggs	arraultzarik	ahr-ROWLTS-ah-reek
cheese	gaztarik	GAHS-tah-reek
I am vegetarian.	Begetarianoa nalz.	beh-geh-tah-ree-AH-noh-ah nahls
Please	Mezedez	mehs-EH-dehs
Thank you	Eskerrik asko	eh-SKAYR-rihk AH-skoh

The food of small, mountainous **Andorra** is largely oriented towards meat. There are both French and Spanish/Catalonian influences in the cuisine, but Andorra's status as a tourist mecca ensures that a variety of cuisines are represented (notably the regrettable "international cuisine" of resort areas). Catalan is the official language, but both French (p. 66) and Castillian Spanish are widely spoken.

Gibraltar, a British colony, offers seafood and rather undistinguished fast food, fish and chips, and "John Bull"-themed pubs. English is spoken everywhere in this tiny colony (although most people can speak Spanish too).

C. CENTRAL AND EASTERN EUROPE

Central and Eastern Europeans generally combine a love for meat with an economic inability to pay for large quantities of it. This combination poses a double threat to vegetarians. First, meat is likely to launch a surprise attack, appearing not as an obvious slab of beef but as a hunk of ham bone in your soup. Second, puzzled, frustrated carnivores may misunderstand you, or worse, treat you as a fool, a dilettante, or a religious freak. Another problem is that to some extent, the concept "meatless" is different here than in the rest of Europe: If a dish is not *mostly* meat, it may be considered *not* meat.

Fortunately, this situation is slowly changing, especially among young people. While there are still few specialty vegetarian restaurants in this part of the world, many ordinary restaurants (especially in urban areas) are beginning to offer meatless entrees, and somewhat less derision is being aimed at people who request them. Many Eastern European countries actually have a long tradition of meatless cooking during Eastern Orthodox fasts. During Orthodox Easter and at certain other times (in some cases totaling half the year), meat was forbidden for religious reasons, and a whole range of grain, vegetable, and legume dishes developed (the consumption of which sometimes extended to people of other religions). You would be lucky to find these dishes offered in restaurants today, but they do exist. As a final option, you may want to look out for "milk bars" (lacto-vegetarian restaurants). Milk bars were common during the Communist era in many Eastern Bloc countries, and some are still in operation today.

Albania

Albanian food is not the most interesting cuisine in the world, nor is it particularly vegetarian-friendly. Meat (or fish, along the coast) is the standard restaurant entree. Vegetarians will be more interested in the typically bland accompaniments, usually boiled vegetables or potatoes. Because of the proximity of Italy and Greece, both pasta and Greek salad are common dishes, and pizza is becoming popular. Although Albania is predominately Muslim, there are many Albanian grain and legume dishes that were originally created for the Eastern Orthodox fasting periods. These dishes can sometimes be found in restaurants in the countryside.

Albanian, spoken in several different dialects, is the principal language. Many Albanians have learned Italian from watching Italian television.

Albanian

In Albania, a nod means no; shaking one's head side to side means yes.

I would like something without ____.	Unë dëshiroj diçka pa ____.	oon duh-shih-roy DEECH-kah pah ____.
We would like something without ____.	Ne dëshirojme diçka pa ____.	neh duh-shih-roym DEECH-kah pah ____.
I do not eat ____.	Unë nuk ha ____.	oon nook kah ____.
I eat ____ and ____.	Unë ha ____ dhe ____.	oon hah ____ thuh ____.
meat	mish	meesh
chicken	pulë	pool
fish	peshk	pehshk
eggs	vezë	vehz
cheese	djathë	dyahth
I am a vegetarian.	Unë jam vegjetarian.	oon yahm veh-gyeh-tah-ree-uhn
Please	Te lutem	teh loot-ehm
Thank you	Faleminderit	fah-leh-meen-deh-reet

Belarus

To most Belarusians, vegetarianism remains an extremely foreign, almost incomprehensible idea; veganism is utterly beyond the pale. A very few restaurants in the cities serve vegetarian entrees. Away from these anomalous establishments, the vegetarian traveler probably will have to make due with vegetable side dishes. The range of options is much like that available in Russia: Potato concoctions, such as potato pancakes, and other root vegetables (primarily parsnips and beets) are the most common items. Fresh fruit and green vegetables make fairly rare appearances in most restaurants, even in the summer. Bread and dairy products such as curds and *kefir* (a liquid, yogurt-like substance) are fairly good, and can provide the centerpiece of a non-vegan diet if all else fails.

Russian (p. 100) is understood everywhere. The traditional national language is Belarusian, but most people use Russian even in everyday conversation. Indeed, many ethnic Belarusians can speak only Russian.

Bosnia and Herzegovina

As in most of the former Yugoslav republics, the range of options available to vegetarians in Bosnia and Herzegovina is limited. Balkan cuisine rarely works wonders with meatless ingredients, and the recent civil war did not make for beneficial culinary innovation. There are some interesting noodle dishes available, and items like pizza, pasta, and salad are common, but most entrees contain meat. Side dishes will probably have to suffice for most vegetarians here.

There are some regional differences in cuisine; Serbian areas are likely to have the sort of dishes available in Serbia, Croatian areas will have typical Croatian dishes, while the Bosnian Muslims will eat dishes from both areas as well as some (usually meat-based) concoctions of their own. Interesting grain- and lentil-based dishes are sometimes available. Before the war, Sarajevo offered the most cosmopolitan selection of cuisine in the region, and if it succeeds fully in rebuilding it is likely to offer it again. When local fresh produce is available, it tends to be of excellent quality.

Serbian (p. 101) and **Croatian** (p. 83) are the main languages in Bosnia and Herzegovina. Once upon a time, not so very long ago, these were considered the same language—Serbo-Croatian. Political realities have intruded, however, so ethnic Croatians now speak Croatian, ethnic Serbs say they speak Serbian, and Bosnian Muslims speak one or the other (although in reality, there is little difference). Some linguists have identified a distinct Bosnian dialect, which uses words that are unique and totally distinct from Serbian or Croatian.

Bulgaria

Although some Bulgarians are vegetarians for health reasons—they are sick and are under doctor's orders to abstain from meat—and there are some restaurants that cater to these invalids, vegetarianism in general is uncommon in Bulgaria. Most main dishes in ordinary restaurants contain meat in varying amounts. However, it is possible to make do on side dishes and appetizers. Baked eggplant (aubergine) or another vegetable, sometimes stuffed with meat or cheese, is a common accompaniment. Bulgarians make a variety of interesting hot or cold vegetable soups, but these are sometimes made with meat stock or lard. It is very easy to get salads, especially *shopska salada*, a cucumber salad with feta, tomatoes, olive oil, and peppers. There are also some interesting traditional dishes made with grains, lentils, and nuts; these are now quite uncommon outside of the home and one would be lucky to find them in a restaurant.

It should be a simple matter to get along by preparing your own food if you choose. Yogurt (*kiselo mlyako*) is available everywhere and is justly renowned. In season, Bulgaria produces a wide array of fruits and vegetables. Bulgarian cheese, which is a white feta-like product made from cow or sheep milk, is also widely available. If self-catering becomes tiresome, in the large cities and the Black Sea resorts there are restaurants serving various European or Asian cuisines, and meatless entrees are sometimes available at these establishments. Snack stands and fast-food restaurants might occasionally offer something edible; pizza is an especially popular snack in Bulgaria, as is *banitsa*, a pastry with a cheese filling (although meat is sometimes used).

Bulgarian is the national language. Russian is the most common second language. The following phrases have been transliterated from the Cyrillic alphabet.

Bulgarian

In Bulgaria, a nod means no; shaking one's head side to side means yes.

I would like something without _____. (female speaker)	Az bih iskala nešto bez _____.	ahz bee IHSS-kah-lahNEH-shtoh behz _____.

I would like something without ____. (male speaker)	Az bih iskal nešto bez ____.	ahz bee IHSS-kahl NEH-shtoh behz ____.
We would like something without ____.	Nie bihme iskali nešto bez ____.	nee BEE-meh IHSS-kah-lee NEH-shtoh behz ____.
I do not eat ____.	Az ne jam ____.	ahz neh yahm ____.
I eat ____ and ____.	Az jam ____ i ____.	ahz yahm ____ ee ____.
meat	meso	meh-SOH
chicken	pile	pee-LAY
fish	riba	REE-bah
eggs	jaitse	yai-TZEH
cheese	sirene	SEE-reh-neh
I am a vegetarian. (male speaker)	Az sâm vegetarianets.	ahz suhm veh-geh-tah-ree-AH-nehtz
I am a vegetarian. (female speaker)	Az sâm vegetarianka.	ahz suhm veh-geh-tah-ree-AHN-kah
Please	Mola	MOH-lah
Thank you	Blagodarja	blah-goh-dahr-YAH

Croatia

The options available to vegetarian visitors in Croatia are quite limited. There are a few vegetarian restaurants in Zagreb, but most restaurants are not particularly geared to providing meatless entrees. Italian food is fairly common, particularly along the coast, so pizza and pasta are options in many areas. (Italian food in Croatia sometimes undergoes odd transformations, such as pizza topped with sour cream.) There are also occasional surprises such as Chinese restaurants, which tend to serve at least one or two vegetarian entrees. A few traditional Croatian main dishes are made without meat, but these dishes are usually found only as part of home-cooked meals.

A more reliable strategy for vegetarians is to focus on side dishes, snacks, or *meze* (appetizers). One common example of *meze* is *ajvar*—a roasted pepper (capsicum) and eggplant (aubergine) spread. Along the Dalmatian coast, *blitva* (chard) sauteed in garlic with new potatoes is a common side dish. Typical snacks are *burek*, a pastry that is usually filled with cheese (but sometimes with meat) or pancakes (including interesting varieties such as spinach pancakes). There are also good bakeries, and fresh produce in the summer and fall is of high quality. Fish is usually the main dish along the coast, so pesco-vegetarians would do well to flock towards the Adriatic.

Croatian, formerly thought of as Serbo-Croatian, is the national language.

Croatian

I would like something without _____. (female speaker)	Željela bih nešto bez ____.	ZHEHL-yeh-luh bee NEHSH-toh behz ____.
I would like something without _____. (male speaker)	Želio bih nešto bez ____.	ZHEH-lee-oh bee NEHSH-toh behz ____.
We would like something without _____.	Željeli bih nešto bez ____.	ZHEHL-yeh-lee bee NEHSH-toh behz ____.
meat	mesa	MEH-sah
chicken	piletine	PEE-leh-tih-neh

fish	ribe	RREE-beh
eggs	jaja	yah-yah
cheese	sira	SEE-rah
I do not eat _____.	Ne jedem _____.	neh YEH-dehm _____.
I eat _____ and _____.	Jedem _____ i _____.	YEH-dehm _____ ee _____.
meat	meso	MEH-soh
chicken	piletinu	PEE-leh-tih-noo
fish	ribu	RREE-boo
eggs	jaje	yah-yeh
cheese	sir	seer
I am a vegetarian. (female speaker)	Ja sam vegetarijanka.	yah sahm veh-geh-tah-ree-YAHN-kuh
I am a vegetarian. (male speaker)	Ja sam vegetarijanac.	yah sahm veh-geh-tah-ree-YAH-nahtz
Please	Molim	MOH-leem
Thank you	Hvala	HVAH-lah

Czech Republic

Although vegetarianism remains uncommon here, it is becoming easier to manage; indeed, the Czech Republic is probably the easiest (or more accurately, the least difficult) of the former Soviet satellites in which to practice vegetarianism. Of course, the normal Czech diet involves meat and plenty of it. Traditionally, Czechs consumed lots of potatoes, and flour or potato dumplings were and are an ubiquitous dish. But the range of options (for

Czechs as well as for visitors) has diversified significantly since the Velvet Revolution. Prague has suffered the onslaught of American fast food, but as a counterpoint several specialty vegetarian restaurants have opened, and there are a burgeoning number of new, vegetarian-friendly restaurants. Restaurants run by or catering to foreigners tend to be especially receptive to vegetarians. (Veganism remains very difficult, however.) Many ordinary restaurants in Prague and Brno now feature a meatless section on the menu.

Outside the cities, obtaining vegetarian meals becomes more difficult. In medium-sized and small cities, some restaurants have begun to offer vegetarian entrees; in small towns and villages, however, choices are few. It is often possible to ask for a special meatless meal, and proprietors are likely to be somewhat more receptive to such requests than they would have been just a few years ago. (Be warned that the quality of the resulting entree may not be stellar.) Otherwise, potato and vegetable side dishes will have to suffice. For those who are unconcerned about fat or cholesterol content, fried breaded cheese (*smazeny sýr*) is on virtually every menu. Pesco-vegetarians should be able to get by with ease in most parts of the Czech Republic.

Czech is the national language. German is widely spoken, especially in the western part of the country. English is becoming a popular second language.

Czech

I would like something without _____. (male speaker)	Rád bych něco bez _____.	rahd bee**kh** NYEH-tzoh behz _____.
I would like something without _____. (female speaker)	Ráda bych něco bez _____.	RAH-dah bee**kh** NYEH-tzoh behz _____.
We would like something without _____.	Rádi bychom něco bez _____.	RAHD-yee BEE-**kh**ohm NYEH-tzoh behz _____.
meat	masa	MUH-suh

chicken	kuřete	KOOR-zheh-teh
fish	ryby	RIH-bih
eggs	vajec	VAH-yehtz
cheese	sýra	SEE-ruh
I do not eat _____.	Nejím _____.	NEH-yeem _____.
I eat _____ and _____.	Jím _____ a _____.	yeem _____ uh _____.
meat	maso	MUH-soh
chicken	kuřata	KOOR-zhuh-tuh
fish	ryby	RIH-bih
eggs	vejce	VAY-tzeh
cheese	sýr	seer
I am a vegetarian. (male speaker)	Jsem vegetarián.	sehm VEH-geh-tuh-ree-ann
I am a vegetarian. (female speaker)	Jsem vegetariánka.	sehm VEH-geh-tuh-ree-ann-kuh
Please	Prosím	PROH-seem
Thank you	Děkuji	DYEH-kuh-yee
We thank you	Děkujeme	DYEH-kuh-yeh-meh

Estonia

Of the three Baltic states, Estonia is probably the most accommodating (or the least hostile) to vegetarians. There are several vegetarian or veggie-friendly restaurants in Talinn, and a few restaurants in other cities are beginning to add the occasional meatless entree to their menus. Pizza is a common snack. Estonians make interesting grain dishes, such as porridges, as well as a variety of fruit or vegetable soups. (Although some soups are made with stock, others are milk-based.) These dishes are only infrequently available in restaurants, however. Similarly, Estonians often collect berries, mushrooms, and other forest produce for use at home, but these items are rarely seen at restaurants. Salads and pasta are often available. However, in many places, vegetarians will have to rely on bread or on the potato side dishes that inevitably accompany every meal. Summer and fall produce and Estonian dairy products are very good. Pesco-vegetarians should have no problems—Estonians eat huge amounts of fish, mostly herring.

Estonian is the official language. Almost a third of the population speaks Russian (p. 100) as a mother tongue, and Latvian and Lithuanian are also occasionally useful.

Estonian

I would like something without _____.	Ma sooviksin midagi ilma _____.	mah soo-VIHK-sihn mih-DAH-gih IHL-mah _____.
meat	lihata	LEE-hah-tah
chicken	kanata	KAH-nah-tah
fish	kalata	KAH-lah-tah
eggs	munata	MOO-nah-tah
cheese	juusttuta	YOOST-too-tah
I do not eat _____.	Ma ei sőő _____.	mah eye soor _____.
I eat _____ and _____.	Ma sőőn _____ ja _____.	mah soorn _____ yaa _____.
meat	liha	LEE-hah

chicken	kana	KAH-nah
fish	kala	KAH-lah
eggs	muna	MOO-nah
cheese	juustu	YOOST-too
I am a vegetarian.	Ma olen taimetoitlane.	mah oh-LAAN tye-meh-TOH-iht-lah-neh
Please	Palun	PAH-loon
Thank you	Tănan	TAAN-aan

Hungary

Hungarian food is widely regarded as among the richest and most inventive in all Europe. Although Hungarians have largely restricted their culinary inventiveness to meat-based dishes such as *goulash*, vegetarians will not necessarily go hungry in Hungary. In Budapest, it has become relatively easy to avoid meat. Some specialty vegetarian restaurants have opened in the last few years, and many restaurants are now beginning to offer meatless entrees. Budapest also has an impressive concentration of pizzerias, which can usually provide vegetarian sustenance. Away from Budapest, the pickings become slimmer. Some Hungarian vegetable side dishes are excellent (but beware of overzealous cooks smothering them in lard). Hungarian soups tend to be excellent, although even non-meat soups are frequently made with meat stock. Traditional chilled fruit soups are generally (but not always) milk-based. Pesco-vegetarians will find that fish is quite common, and is especially good along Lake Balaton.

Hungarian is the national language.

Hungarian

I would like	Szeretnék kérni	seh-reht-NAYK KAYR-nee
something	valamit ____ nélkül.	vah-lah-MEET ____
without ____.		NAYL-kewl.

We would like something without ___.	Szeretnék kérni valamit ___ nélkül.	seh-reht-NAYNK KAYR-nee vah-lah-MEET ___ NAYL-kewl.
meat	hús	hoosh
chicken	csirke	CHEER-keh
fish	hal	hahl
eggs	tojás	TOY-ahsh
cheese	sajt	shoyt
I do not eat ___.	Nem eszem ___.	naym EH-sehm ___.
I eat ___ and ___.	Eszem ___ és ___.	EH-sehm ___ aysh ___.
meat	húst	hoosht
chicken	csirkét	CHEER-kayt
fish	halat	hah-laht
eggs	tojást	TOH-yahsht
cheese	sajtot	shoy-toht
I am a vegetarian.	Vegetáriánus vagyok.	vay-guh-tah-ree-ah-noosh vahd-YOHK
Please	Kérek	KAY-rehk
Thank you	Köszönöm	kuhr-suhr-nuhm

Latvia

The average Latvian diet is heavy on meat and potatoes. There are a few restaurants in Riga that serve vegetarian entrees, but these are definitely unusual. Pesco-vegetarians will get by easily, as fresh or smoked fish and eel are easy to find. Strict vegetarians may struggle. At home, most Latvians cook with whole grains such as buckwheat, oats, or barley, but dishes made with such wholesome ingredients are hard to find in restaurants. As elsewhere in the Baltic states, potatoes in one form or another are popular both at home and in restaurants. Other sturdy vegetables, particularly root crops, are standard Latvian fare. Some grain or vegetable soups, such as barley soup or *biešu* (borscht), may entice, but these are often made with meat stock.

If you rely on your own initiative and cooking skills, life will be relatively easy. Wonderful fruit and vegetables are available in summer, and apples are abundant in the fall. (Preserved produce is sometimes available during the rest of the year.) Latvia produces good breads and other baked goods, and dairy products such as cheese, cottage cheese, and yogurt are both of high quality and easily available. As Latvia progresses economically and gets more exposure to the outside world, vegetarianism will no doubt become easier to practice and more accepted.

Latvian is the official language. A substantial minority of the population speaks Russian (p. 100) as a first language, and most people can speak it as a second language.

Latvian

I would like something without _____.	Es gribētu pasūtīt kautko bez _____.	ehss GREE-bah-too PAH-soo-teet KOWT-koh behz _____.
We would like something without _____.	Mēs vēlamies pasūtīt kautko bez _____.	mayss VAH-luh-mees PAH-soo-teet KOWT-koh behz _____.
meat	gaļas	GAHL-luhss
chicken	vistas	VISS-tahss

fish	zivs	zihvs
eggs	olām	OH-lahm
cheese	siera	SEE-eh-ruh
I do not eat _____.	Es neēdu _____.	ehss NAY-ah-doo _____.
I eat _____ and _____.	Es ēdu _____ un _____.	ehss AH-doo _____ uhn _____.
meat	gaļu	GAHL-loo
chicken	vistu	VISS-too
fish	zivi	ZEE-vee
eggs	olas	OO-wuh-luhss
cheese	sieru	SEE-eh-roo
Please	Lūdzu	LOOD-zoo
Thank you	Paldies	pahl-DEE-uhs

Lithuania

Despite some incremental improvements in recent years (and the recent opening of a few vegetarian restaurants), it remains quite difficult to find meatless meals in Lithuania. Part of the problem is misunderstanding: For example, many so-called "vegetarian" pizzas are made with ham. Another part of the problem is resentment bred from years of deprivation, which causes otherwise friendly and rational people to view vegetarianism as new age, self-indulgent, insulting behavior. This general hostility is particularly unfortunate because Lithuanians make some very good traditional meatless food. Mushrooms, berries, and other forest produce constitute traditional ingredients in many homemade Lithuanian dishes, but these are rarely available in restaurants. Porridges and vegetable soups provide another meatless option, but again, these are hard to find outside of homes.

Boiled potatoes accompany most main dishes in restaurants. There are a whole host of more elaborate potato dishes such as pancakes and dumplings, but many of these are mixed with some form of meat. Pasta and really excellent breads are easily available, and salads are becoming more common than they once were. If you cook for yourself, local fruit and vegetables are wonderful in season. Pesco-vegetarians should have no problems here: Fish, especially herring, is ubiquitous.

Lithuanian is the official language. Russian (p. 100) is widely spoken as a second language, and the Russian ethnic minority within the country speaks it as a first language. There is also a Polish-speaking minority.

Lithuanian

I would like something without ____.	Aš norėčiau ką nors be ____.	uhsh noh-REH-chow kah nohrrs beh ____.
We would like something without ____.	Mes norėtumėm ką nors be ____.	mahs noh-REH-tuh-mehm kah nohrrs beh ____.
meat	mėsos	MAY-sohs
chicken	vištienos	vihsh-TYEH-nohs
fish	žuvies	zhoo-VEES
eggs	kiaušinių	kee-ow-SHINN-yoo
cheese	sūrio	SOO-rih-oh
I do not eat ____.	Aš nevalgau ____.	uhsh neh-VUHL-gow ____.
I eat ____ and ____.	Aš valgau ____ ir ____.	uhsh VUHL-gow ____ ihr ____.
meat	mėsą	MAY-sah
chicken	vištieną	vihsh-TYEH-nah

fish	žuvį	ZHOO-vee
eggs	kiaušinius	kee-ow-SHINN-yuhs
cheese	sūrį	SOO-ree
I am a vegetarian. (male speaker)	Aš esu vegetaras.	uhsh eh-SOO veh-geh-TAH-ruhs
I am a vegetarian. (female speaker)	Aš esu vegetarė.	uhsh eh-SOO veh-geh-TAH-ray
Please.	Prašau	prahsh-OW
Thank you.	Ačiu	AH-choo

Macedonia

Although some meatless food is available, Macedonia remains a difficult place to find vegetarian meals. For economic reasons, most Macedonians tend to avoid using much meat at home. This vegetarianism is generally forced, not intentional; very few people here are vegetarians by choice. Most restaurants specialize in meat, reasoning that their patrons usually eat vegetarian food at home and are looking for a change. However, there are often interesting vegetable side dishes available. Some of these dishes are the result of Turkish or Greek influence: Greek salads, eggplant (aubergine), and cheese or spinach pastries are all fairly typical. The few restaurants that are used to foreigners are more likely to offer meatless entrees. Pizza is a common snack food, and pasta is sometimes available at restaurants. Self-caterers are likely to be favorably impressed with the quality of Macedonian produce in season.

Macedonian is the main national language. Macedonia uses both the Cyrillic and the Roman alphabet, although Cyrillic is more commonly used. A large minority of the population speaks Albanian (p. 79). Serbian is also widely spoken, and is the most common second language.

Macedonian

I would like something without _____. (male speaker)	Bi sakal nešto bez _____.	bee SAH-kahl NEHSH-toh behz _____.
I would like something without _____. (female speaker)	Bi sakala nešto bez _____.	bee SAH-kah-lah NEHSH-toh behz _____.
We would like something without _____.	Bi sakale nešto bez _____.	bee SAH-kah-leh NEHSH-toh behz _____.
I do not eat _____.	Ne jadam _____.	neh YAH-dahm _____.
I eat _____ and _____.	Jadam _____ i _____.	YAH-dahm ___ ee _____.
meat	meso	MEH-soh
chicken	kokoška	KOH-kohsh-kah
fish	riba	REE-bah
eggs	jajca	yai-tsah
cheese	sirenje	SEE-reh-neh
I am a vegetarian. (male speaker)	Jas sum vegetarijanec.	yahss soom veh-geh-tah-ree-YAH-nehts
I am a vegetarian. (female speaker)	Jas sum vegetarijanka.	yahss soom veh-geh-tah-ree-YAHN-kah
Please	Molam	MOH-lahm
Thank you	Blagodaram	blah-GOH-dah-rahm

Moldova

Despite (or because of) their relative poverty, few Moldovans are willing vegetarians, and many common dishes contain pieces of meat in some form. Nonetheless, it is possible to subsist on Moldova's national dish, *mamalagia*, an orange (ground maize) mush similar to polenta. (Sometimes bits of meat or meat stock is added.) It is usually served with meat or vegetable stew or feta cheese. Sometimes fried vegetables are available, and pasta and pizza are occasionally found. Upscale restaurants are more likely (though not guaranteed) to have vegetarian options. A variety of vegetable soups appear on menus, but these are often made with meat stock. Bread is quite good and very hearty, and Moldovan produce is excellent when it is available.

Moldovan is the official language. It is virtually identical to **Romanian** (p. 98) in all important respects. Russian is also widely spoken. A small minority of the population speaks a Turkish dialect.

Poland

Poland has a long list of traditional dishes that are prepared without meat, and instead contain mushrooms and other forest produce, grains such as buckwheat, or pulses such as lentils. These dishes can be hard to find at restaurants, however; as Poland grows wealthier, traditional food is often maligned as "peasant food" and meat consumption is skyrocketing after years of rationing and privation. Indeed, many Poles (predominantly older people) find vegetarianism as a conscious choice to be an utterly incomprehensible concept. At the same time, however, vegetarianism is becoming more common, especially among young people. Warsaw, Krakow, and other large cities now have vegetarian restaurants; many ordinary restaurants in urban areas, particularly more upscale establishments, are adding vegetarian entrees to their menus. The cities also offer some ethnic choices, such as Chinese restaurants. Salad bars are becoming popular (but watch out for meat in salads).

Outside the cities, it is difficult to find meatless entrees. Some towns still have milk bars (dairy restaurants) left over from the Communist era, but these are closing. Pizza is a common snack food, but Polish pizza tends to be appalling. Soups are sometimes a good option, although they are often made with stock or may even contain bits of meat. Polish borscht is usually vegetarian (unlike the versions served in the former Soviet Union). Starchy side dishes may come to the rescue; potatoes and potato pancakes are very common, and some *pierogi* (dumplings) are meatless. Yogurt and other dairy products are widely available.

Polish is the national language. Russian is the most common second language. Some English is spoken in the cities, but it is not widely spoken in rural areas.

Polish

I would like something without ____.	Proszę coś bez ____.	PROH-shehn tsohsh behz ____.
We would like something without ____.	Prosimy coś bez ____.	proh-SHEE-mih oh tsohsh behz ____.
I do not eat ____.	Nie jem ____.	nyeh yehm ____.
meat	mięsa	mee-EHN-sah
chicken	kury	KOO-rih
fish	ryby	rrih-bih
eggs	jajek	yai-YEK
cheese	sera	sehr
I eat ____ and ____.	Jem ____ i ____.	yehm ____ ee ____.
meat	mięso	mee-EHN-soh
chicken	kurę	KOO-rreh
fish	ryby	rrih-bih

eggs	jajka	yai-KAH
cheese	ser	sehr
I am a vegetarian. (male speaker)	Jestem wegetarianinem.	YEH-stehm veh-geh-tah-rree-ah-NIHN-ehm
I am a vegetarian. (female speaker)	Jestem wegetarianiną.	YEH-stehm veh-geh-tah-rree-ah-NIHN-ah**n**
Please	Proszę	PROH-sheh**n**
Thank you	Dziękuję	jyeh**n**-KOO-yeh**n**

Romania

Meat is too expensive for the average Romanian to eat on a daily basis, so the majority of Romanians are unwilling vegetarians. Those who can afford to eat out generally go "whole hog" for meat. Nonetheless, most resturants that cater to tourists (generally more pricey establishments) offer vegetarian entrees. Romania formerly had many lacto-vegetarian restaurants serving, as the name implies, meatless food that often included dairy products. These restaurants were originally meant for people who were on a meatless diet by doctor's orders. Most are now private enterprises that serve meat, although some meatless dishes can still be had.

At ordinary restaurants the choices for vegetarians are limited. There are plenty of vegetable soups and stews, but these usually use meat stock or contain bits of meat. Pasta is reasonably common. The most distinctive Romanian dish is probably *mamalgia*, (ground maize) mush served with cheese or milk. It should be noted that many practicing Christian Romanians avoid meat, and sometimes all animal products, two days per week throughout the year, and for weeks at a time during Lent, the pre-Christmas period, and parts of June and August. Monasteries serve meatless (sometimes entirely vegan) dishes at these times. Some restaurants may also be accommodating to vegetarians during these periods.

The official language is **Romanian**; a Romance language, it sits forlornly among the Slavic languages of Eastern Europe. The Hungarian ethnic minority speaks Hungarian (p. 88).

Romanian

I would like something without _____.	Asi dori ceva fără _____.	ahsh doh-REE jeh-VAAH FUH-ruh _____.
We would like something without _____.	Am dori ceva fără _____.	ahm doh-REE jeh-VAAH FUH-ruh _____.
I do not eat _____.	Nu mănânc _____.	noo MUH-newnk _____.
I eat _____ and _____.	Mănânc _____ şi _____.	MUH-newnk _____ shee _____.
meat	carne	KAHR-nay
chicken	pui	pwee
fish	peşte	PAYSH-tay
eggs	ouă	OH-wuh
cheese	brânză	BREWN-zuh
I am a vegetarian. (male speaker)	Sunt vegetarian.	soont veh-jeh-tah-ree-yahn
I am a vegetarian. (female speaker)	Sunt vegetariană.	soont veh-jeh-tah-ree-yah-nuh
Please	Vă rog	vuh rohg
Thank you	Mulţumesc	mool-tsoo-MEHSK

Russia

Russians tell an old joke that goes, "All Russians are vegetarians! We have no meat, no milk, no eggs . . ." While privation and shortages have taken a toll on Russian meat consumption, very few Russians are intentional vegetarians, and most think the concept is exceedingly strange. Most restaurants have no meatless entrees at all, and since the few dishes that do not contain meat usually contain dairy products instead, vegans are in a dire situation. However, attitudes are slowly changing. Many Russians now understand the concept of vegetarianism, even if they do not appreciate it; young people in urban areas are most likely to be receptive to the idea. In Moscow and St. Petersburg, a few vegetarian restaurants have opened up, and some ordinary restaurants have begun to experiment with meatless entrees. Many of the Western chains that have opened in Russia in the last few years serve vegetarian dishes. There are also a few ethnic restaurants in the large cities serving Chinese, Vietnamese, Middle Eastern, or other cuisines; Georgian or Armenian restaurants are highly regarded, and almost always offer some wonderful meatless entrees. Western European cuisines are also well-represented, but these restaurants tend to be expensive.

Outside the major cities, vegetarian prospects become bleak. There is surprisingly little variation in the type of food available, except in the Caucasus where local cooking becomes more interesting. Potatoes are served as part of almost every meal. Vegetables are usually canned. There are some good soups, but they are typically made with meat stock. (Even *borscht* is generally meat-based.) However, some fruit soups do not contain stock. Cucumber salad, combined with *zakuski* (appetizers), could make a meal. Omelettes are often available, and buckwheat porridge or pancakes can sometimes be found. Dairy products are more easily available than they once were; *kefir*, yogurt, curds, and cheese are all relatively common and nutritious. Russian bread is also filling and generally good.

Away from the few urban centers, Siberia poses a special challenge. Almost everything contains meat, and fresh vegetables are rare; even canned vegetables are not always available. It is probably best to cook for oneself here. The situation is considerably ameliorated for pesco-vegetarians: Fish is common in most of Siberia, as well as in the remainder of Russia.

Russian is the official language. There are hordes of minority groups in Russia, especially in the Caucasus, Siberia, and Tatarstan, which speak their own language as a mother tongue. Almost everyone can speak Russian as a second language, however. Languages listed elsewhere in this book that may come in handy in Russia include Armenian (p. 116), Georgian (p. 119),

Azeri (p. 117), Uzbek (p. 197), Kazakh (p. 192), Ukrainian (p. 107), or Mongolian (p. 204).

Russian

The following phrases have been transliterated from the Cyrillic alphabet.

I /We would like something without _____.	Možno što nibud´ bez _____.	MAWZH-naw SHTAW nee-bood byehz _____.
meat	mjasa	MYAH-suh
chicken	kuritsi	koo-reets-ee
fish	ribi	RRIH-bih
eggs	jaits	yah-eets
cheese	sira	seer-uh
I do not eat _____.	Ja nje kušaju _____.	yah nyeh KOO-shah-yoo _____.
I eat _____ and _____.	Ja kušaju _____ i _____.	yah KOO-shah-yoo _____ ee _____.
meat	mjaso	MYAH-saw
chicken	kuritsu	koo-reets-oo
fish	ribu	RRIH-boo
eggs	jaitsa	yah-eets-uh
cheese	sir	seer
I am a vegetarian. (male speaker)	Ja vjegjetjarianjetz.	yah vyeh-gyeh-tyeh-ree-AH-nyehtz

I am a vegetarian. (female speaker)	Ja vjegjetjerianka.	yah vyeh-gyeh-tyeh-ree-AHN-kuh
Please	Požalujsta	paw-ZHAHL-stahh
Thank you	Spasibo	spah-SEE-baw

Serbia and Montenegro

A common term for Serbia and Montenegro, "rump Yugoslavia," largely sums up the dietary options in this part of the world. Of all former Yugoslav republics, Serbia and Montenegro are probably the least tuned in to the outside world. Most people are unlikely to understand the concept of vegetarianism, which is considered bizarre and unhealthy. A few restaurants are beginning to add meatless dishes to their menus, but these are exceptions. The few common meatless options usually take the form of side dishes; these include salads, grilled mushrooms, and the occasional fried or roasted vegetable dish. Most towns have pizzerias, and many restaurants offer pizza or pasta (you will have to tell them you do not want meat). There are also some traditional noodle and pastry dishes that do not contain meat, and are often delicious. These dishes are frequently available at snack stands or hole-in-the-wall establishments. Dairy products and bread tend to be adequate and readily available. In season, there is excellent local produce, but usually you will have to prepare it yourself—most restaurants inexplicably fail to take advantage of this local bounty.

Serbian is the national language. Although there are some minor differences, it is essentially the same as Croatian (p. 83). Most parts of Serbia use the Cyrillic alphabet; in Montenegro, Roman script is sometimes used. Albanian (p. 79) is the majority language in Kosovo province.

Serbian

The following phrases have been transliterated from the Cyrillic alphabet.

I would like something without _____. (male speaker)	Željeo bih nešto bez _____.	ZHEH-leh-oh bee NEHSH-toh behz _____.

I would like something without _____. (female speaker)	Želela bih nešto bez _____.	ZHEH-leh-lah bee NEHSH-toh behz _____.
We would like something without _____.	Želeli bih nešto bez _____.	ZHEH-leh-lee bee NEHSH-toh behz _____.
meat	mesa	MEH-sah
chicken	piletine	PEE-leh-tee-neh
fish	ribe	REE-beh
eggs	jaja	yah-yah
cheese	sira	SEE-rah
I do not eat _____.	Ne jedem ___.	neh YEH-dehm _____.
I eat _____ and _____.	Jedem ____ i ____.	YEH-dehm ____ ee ____.
meat	meso	MEH-saw
chicken	piletinu	PEE-leh-tee-noo
fish	ribu	RREE-boo
eggs	jaja	yah-yah
cheese	sir	seer
I am a vegetarian. (male speaker)	Ja sam vegetarijanats.	yah sahm veh-geh-tah-REE-yah-nahtz
I am a vegetarian. (female speaker)	Ja same vegetarijanka.	yah sahm veh-geh-tah-REE-yahn-kuh

| **Please** | Molim | MOH-leem |
| **Thank you** | Hvala | HVAH-lah |

Slovakia

In Slovakia, meat is the core of a restaurant lunch or dinner, and vegetarianism is rare (although the average Slovak eats little meat at home due to the expense). The hapless diner may be greeted by slabs of beef or pork, or sometimes fish. Despite the general dearth of meatless entrees, there are a couple of vegetarian restaurants in Bratislava, and a few other restaurants are beginning to offer vegetarian entrees (primarily restaurants that cater to foreigners in touristed areas). Away from these veggie-friendly oases, a visiting vegetarian may have to subsist on potatoes or other vegetable side dishes, perhaps (if you are lucky) accompanied by beans or lentils. The Slovak national dish is a sort of dumpling and cheese concoction called *bryndzové halušky*, but it can be hard to find at restaurants. There also exist a range of potato-based dishes, such as dumplings and potato pancakes; these are commonly served as snacks as well as main dishes. If you cook for yourself, during the summer and fall you will find wonderful fresh produce at local markets. Slovak bread tends to be quite good.

    Slovak is the national language. Although Slovak was often lumped in with Czech before Czechoslovakia split, they are distinct albeit similar languages. Russian is widely spoken as a second language.

Slovak

I would like something without _____. (female speaker)	Chcela by som niečo bez ____.	KEH-seh-lah bih sohm NYEH-choh behz ____.
I would like something without _____. (male speaker)	Chcel by som niečo bez ____.	KEH-sehl bih sohm NYEH-choh behz ____.
We would like something without _____.	Chceli by sme niečo bez ____.	KEH-seh-lih bih smeh NYEH-choh behz ____.

meat	mäsa	MEH-suh
chicken	kurčata	KOO-chuh-tyuh
fish	rýb	reeb
eggs	vajec	VUH-yehts
cheese	syru	SIH-roo
I do not eat _____.	Nejem _____.	NUH-yehm _____.
I eat _____ and _____.	Jem _____ a _____.	yehm _____ uh _____.
meat	mäso	MEH-soh
chicken	kura	KOO-rah
fish	ryby	REE-bee
eggs	vajcia	VYTES-yuh
cheese	syr	seer
I am a vegetarian. (female speaker)	Som vegetariánka.	sohm VEH-geh-tuh-rih-ahn-kah
I am a vegetarian. (male speaker)	Som vegetarián.	sohm VEH-geh-tuh-rih-ahn
Please	Prosím	PROH-seem
Thank you	Ďakujem	DYUH-kuh-yehm
We thank you	Ďakujeme	DYUH-kuh-yeh-meh

Slovenia

Vegetarianism is not yet common or widely accepted in Slovenia, but it is becoming almost fashionable among young people. Older people are still very resistant to the idea, especially in rural areas; in the countryside, pork fat is often used to cook vegetables and grains, and most people eat as much meat as they can get. Still, Slovenia is probably the easiest of the former Yugoslav states for vegetarians to cope with. A few vegetarian restaurants are starting to crop up, mainly in Ljubljana. There are many pizza restaurants, most of which offer vegetarian pizzas. Some delis and supermarkets sell vegetarian sandwiches. In conventional restaurants, it is usually a simple matter to construct a meal from vegetable side dishes, and many restaurants have pasta dishes. A common Slovenian snack, *burek* (a flaky turnover), is sometimes made with cheese or vegetables instead of meat. On the coast, fish-eaters will find plenty of seafood dishes.

Slovene is the national language. Croatian and German are common second languages. Some Italian is spoken along the coast.

Slovene

I would like something without _____.	Želim jesdi nekaj brez _____.	zheh-LEEM YEHSS-dee nay-kye brehz _____.
We would like something without _____.	Želimo jesdi nakaj brez _____.	zheh-LEEM-oh YEHSS-dee nay-kye brehz _____.
I do not eat _____.	Ne jem _____.	neh yehm _____.
meat	mesa	meh-SAH
chicken	piščanca	pees-CHAHN-tsah
fish	ribe	RRIH-beh
eggs	jajc	yites
cheese	sira	see-rah
I eat _____ and _____.	Jem _____ in _____.	yehm _____ een _____.

meat	meso	meh-SOH
chicken	piščanca	pees-CHAHN-tsah
fish	ribo	RRIH-boh
eggs	jajca	YITE-sah
cheese	sir	seer
I am a vegetarian. (male speaker)	Sem vegeterianec.	suhm veh-geh-teh-ree-YAH-nehtz
I am a vegetarian. (female speaker)	Sem vegetarianka.	suhm veh-geh-tah-re-YAHN-kah
Please	Prosim	PROH-seem
Thank you	Hvala	HVAH-lah

Ukraine

Ukrainians are largely unsympathetic to vegetarians, although this attitude is changing very gradually. Most Ukrainian main dishes contain meat or fish, albeit often in small quantities. Main dishes are usually served with some permutation of potato, whether boiled, made into pancakes, or fashioned into dumplings. Besides the sturdy potato, which may be a vegetarian's best friend in Ukraine, one can find various other grain-based dishes, such as *nalesnyky* (blintzes), buckwheat pancakes, and cheese or vegetable dumplings (the latter are often filled with or smothered by meat). Perhaps the most common grain dish is *kasha*, a substantial grain porridge usually made from buckwheat. Hearty bread is served at every meal. Fresh fruit and vegetables can be hard to find, especially out of season; vegetables are easiest to find in the Crimean region.

Some smaller restaurants in Ukraine may offer traditional meatless specialties (although not from an intentional desire to be vegetarian-friendly). Ukrainian vegetable soups such as *borscht* can be very good, but unfortunately they are usually made with meat broth. For non-vegans, fermented dairy products such as yogurt, *kefir*, or curds are easily available and provide a good way to add variety to the diet.

Ukrainian is the main language. Russian (p. 100) is very widely spoken, and is the first language of the many ethnic Russians who live in southern and eastern Ukraine.

Ukrainian

The following phrases have been trasliterated from the Cyrillic alphabet used to write Ukrainian.

I would like something without _____.	Ja khochi schos' bez _____.	yah khoh-chih sh-chohss behz _____.
I do not eat _____.	Ja ne jim _____.	yah neh yeem _____.
meat	mjasa	MYAH-suh
chicken	kurki	KOORR-kih
fish	ribi	RRIH-bih
eggs	jajets	yai-YEHTS
cheese	siru	SIHR-roo
I eat _____ and _____.	Ja jim _____ i _____.	yah yeem _____ ee _____.
meat	mjaso	MYAH-saw
chicken	kurku	KOOR-koo
fish	ribu	RRIH-boo
eggs	jajtse	yai-TSEH
cheese	sir	seer

I am a vegetarian. (male speaker)	Ja vegetarianets´.	yah veh-heh-tah-ree-AH-nehtz
I am a vegetarian. (female speaker)	Ja vegetarianka.	yah veh-heh-tah-ree-AHN-kuh
Please	Prošu	PROH-shoo
Thank you	Djakyu	DYAH-koo-yoo

North Africa and the Middle East

North Africa and the Middle East share the salient characteristic of being overwhelmingly arid or semi-arid. This factor influences the cuisine of the region in myriad ways. For example, beef and pork are mostly absent—beef for climatic and economic reasons, pork because the region's inhabitants are mainly Muslim or Jewish. Instead, lamb and goat are the most common meats. For vegetarians, this fact simply means that there are generally fewer types of meat to avoid. Similarly, dairy products are not as prevalent as in North America or Europe, although yogurt and goat or sheep (or in some places, camel) milk and cheese are fairly common. The climate also limits the range of crops. Certain kinds of grains, such as wheat or millet, along with legumes like lentils, chickpeas, and kidney beans, form the basis of the diet. Nuts, fruits, and vegetables round out the offerings, particularly in irrigated areas. In many countries throughout the region it is easy to find meatless dishes centered on these basic ingredients.

Substantial variations exist among countries, however. In some countries the average diet is quite Spartan, while in others meat (or fish) in some form almost always accompanies—or smothers—meatless portions. Nonetheless, it is usually possible to find something edible and meatless. Honored guests may have special difficulties: Arab hospitality is legendary, and a visitor may be served a mighty selection of dishes, including some highly unappetizing animal portions. You may be expected to sample (although not necessarily to finish) everything that is placed before you. Not doing so would cause great offense. The only respectable alternative might be to feign a severe allergy (which should not be too difficult with a sheep's eye staring at you).

Language

The dominant language of the region is **Arabic**. Spoken Arabic varies dramatically from one region to another; the Arabic spoken in Morocco will be very different in many respects from the Arabic spoken in Yemen, for example. Nonetheless, the phrases listed below are fairly simple and should be understood by Arabic-speakers throughout North Africa and the Middle East. The local pronunciation may be different, but you will probably sound merely stilted and strange, not totally incomprehensible.

Arabic

The phrases below have been transliterated from the ornate script used to write Arabic.

I would like something without _____.	Ana orid akil biduun _____.	ah-NAH ow-REED AH-keel bee-doon _____.
We would like something without _____.	Ehna norid akil biduun _____.	eh-NAH now-REED AH-keel bee-doon _____.
I do not eat _____.	Ana la akoul _____.	ah-NAH lah AH-kool _____.
I eat _____ and _____.	Ana akoul _____ wa _____.	ah-NAH AH-kool _____ wah _____.
meat	laham	lah-**KH**AM
chicken	dajaj	dah-zhahzh
fish	samak	sah-mahk
eggs	baid	byde
cheese	joubnah	zhihbb-nah

Please		Raja'an	rah-zhah-ahn
	or	Min fadlak	meen FAHD-lahk
Thank you		Shukran	shuh-KRAHN

A. NORTH AFRICA

The countries along the southern rim of the Mediterranean Sea bask in a benefi-
cent climate, and produce wonderful fruits and vegetables. However, most North
Africans have a rather basic diet, the exact substance of which changes as one
moves from west to east. *Couscous*, a dish of semolina or other grains made into
small, pasta-like pieces, is the staple food in the Maghreb (Morocco, Algeria, and
Tunisia). Egypt is more cosmopolitan, with notable Middle Eastern influences.
Vegetarianism is not practiced much in this area, and most North Africans glad-
ly eat meat when they can get it. Nonetheless, it should be possible to avoid meat
in all but the most remote desert areas.

Algeria

Algerian food is similar to that of its neighbors, Morocco and Tunisia:
Couscous is the staple, and meat takes on a supporting role as soup and sauce
ingredient. Some vegetable or lentil-based dishes are available, mainly in the
form of side dishes or appetizers; one common example is *makouda*, made
with eggs, potatoes, parsley, and lentils. Vegetable stews are quite common,
but these are usually made with meat stock. In the Sahara, vegetables become
less common (understandably so!); couscous is usually available, however.
European-style restaurants are scattered throughout the cities of the north;
these often offer at least one meatless entree such as pizza or spaghetti.

   Arabic (p. 110) is the official language. Berber dialects are also spoken.
Many Algerians speak French as a second language.

Egypt

Hearteningly, the Egyptian national dish is *fuul*—fava or kidney beans in a
spicy sauce. Although lamb and other fleshy items such as goose are very
popular, there is a decent variety of meatless food available. Eggplant
(aubergine) dishes, rice with nuts and dried fruit, and Lebanese-style food
such as *falafel, baba ghanoush*, and *hummus* are all common. Another common dish, stuffed grape leaves, is occasionally filled with rice and lentils
instead of meat. Typical snack foods include *sambousek* (pastries filled with
cheese or vegetables) and *fiteer* (a cross between a pastry and pizza, filled with
meat, eggs, or white cheese). Some varieties of vegetable or legume soups do

not contain meat (although they are sometimes made with meat stock). In Cairo and Alexandria, and to a lesser extent in smaller cities and tourist centers, there are plenty of Indian restaurants and restaurants serving European-style food such as pasta.

Arabic (p. 110) is the official language. People who deal with tourists can usually speak English or French (or both).

Libya

Libya is at the crossroads of North Africa, and its food reflects its geographical position. The *fuul* (kidney or fava beans) of Egypt is in evidence, while the couscous of the Maghreb countries is also very popular. Unfortunately, Libyan couscous is sometimes cooked in lamb stock, and is often served with meat sauce. There are some vegetable stews, but these usually have a meat base, or else have unappetizing chunks of lamb or mutton floating in them. A third culinary influence—that of the Italians who colonized and occupied Libya—is apparent in the various permutations of pasta that are widely available.

Arabic (p. 110) is the national language. Italian can be useful, especially with older Libyans, but its use is decreasing as a policy of Arabicization takes hold.

Morocco

Morocco is best known for *couscous* (crushed semolina). While couscous may be a vegetarian's lifesaver in Morocco, it can be hard to find in restaurants—it is usually eaten at home, and in any case is at its best when homemade. Even when couscous is available, it is sometimes served covered in meat sauce or made with meat stock; Moroccans tend to make use of as much meat as they can afford. Another famous Moroccan dish, *tajine* (a kind of stew), usually contains lamb or other meat, but is occasionally meat-free. Other types of soup are frequently made with lamb stock, even if actual chunks of meat are absent. *Harira* (lentil stew) is often meatless. Meatless sandwiches are easy to find. In towns, French-style bakeries, restaurants, and cafes offer another option, although apart from bread, pastries, and sandwiches, the range of meatless offerings can be slim. Good yogurt is easily available in shops and fruit, especially citrus fruit, is ubiquitous.

Arabic (p. 110) is the official language. Berber dialects are spoken in the mountains and in the interior. French is commonly spoken as a second language. Spanish is useful in the far north. Moroccans who deal regularly with tourists are amazing linguists, and are sometimes proficient in seven or eight languages (including English).

Western Sahara, a former Spanish colony, is now under *de facto* Moroccan control. The diet is considerably less varied than in Morocco proper; couscous, fish, and meat are the most common foods. While Arabic is the most common language here, Spanish remains useful.

Tunisia

Of the cuisines of the Maghreb region, Tunisian food displays the most European influence. French bread (plain or stuffed) is served all over Tunisia, and the cities have many French-style cafes and restaurants. Many European-style restaurants serve one or two meatless dishes. Pasta and pizza are extremely common. Because meat is so expensive, the basic diet of most Tunisians consists of grains and legumes, with vegetables or fruit; meat is used only in small amounts. However, Tunisians eat meat with gusto on special occasions, such as at restaurant meals or when a guest is present. Couscous, the Tunisian staple, is available in many varieties, but is often served with meat sauce. Salads, roasted or fried vegetables, and lentil or vegetable soups are all fairly common. Tunisian fruit is outstanding. Along the coast, fish is devoured by all and sundry (except for vegetarians). Several common snack items may be suitable for vegetarians; these include spinach and vegetable turnovers, *briq* (an egg-filled pastry), and *chaksuka* (chopped vegetables and egg). However, these snacks sometimes contain bits of meat.

Arabic (p. 110) is the official language. Most Tunisians can also speak French.

B. THE MIDDLE EAST

Several dishes many vegetarians know and love trace their origins to the Middle East; they include *hummus* (a chickpea-based dip), *tabouli* (a cracked-wheat and vegetable salad), and *falafel* (fried balls of spiced chickpea flour). While these dishes are common in many Middle Eastern countries, the cuisine of the region can be much richer and more complex (and in many cases, less vegetarian-friendly). Some countries in the region, particularly Turkey and the Caucasus nations (Armenia, Georgia, and Azerbaijan), have unique cuisines that are very different from what is normally thought of as Middle Eastern cooking. The countries of the Arabian peninsula place the most importance on meat, and the food can be unrelentingly monotonous. In most cases, though, a vegetarian in the Middle East should be able to find something tasty and meat-free to eat, if only an assortment of appetizers or side dishes.

Armenia

Armenia offers an impressive variety of imaginative vegetarian options. Although few Armenians are full-time vegetarians, most people give up meat, and sometimes all animal products, during Lent and other times of fasting. The dishes crafted to cope with forced periods of meatlessness are so good that they are often available throughout the year. Potential ingredients include bulgur, rice, eggplant (aubergines), chickpeas, and a bountiful array of fruits, vegetables, and nuts. Most dishes are served with a sauce that is based on olive oil or tomato; sometimes the sauce contains dried fruits, almonds, or pine nuts. Omelettes, sheep cheese, flat bread or yeast bread, *boeregs* (turnovers), and a host of *meza* (appetizers) all provide excellent meatless sustenance. One should not forget that many Armenian dishes *do* contain meat, so ordering at random from a menu is not recommended. Still, Armenia remains a relatively easy country for meat-free eating.

Armenian is the national language. Russian can also be useful.

Armenian

The words and phrases below have been transliterated from Armenian script.

I do not eat ____.	Yes chemm ooder ____.	yehss chehm oo-DEHR ____.
I eat ____.	Yes goodem ____.	yehss goo-DEHM ____.
meat	mis	mees
chicken	hav	hahv
fish	dzouk	tsoog
eggs	havkit	hahv-KEET
cheese	baneer	bah-NEER
I am a vegetarian.	Pancharager em.	pahn-chah-rah-GEHR ehm
Please	Hajees	hah-jees
Thank you	Shnoragalem	shuh-nohr-ah-GAH-lehm

Azerbaijan

Unlike its mostly Orthodox Christian neighbors Georgia and Armenia, Azerbaijan is a predominantly Muslim country, and thus lacks the meatless fasting periods that have given rise to the wide variety of vegetarian dishes in those countries. However, with some effort it is perfectly possible to avoid meat. Azerbaijan is the home of rice pilaf, and while this is often served with sides of lamb or other meat, you are certainly under no compulsion to eat the meat. (Pilaf is frequently made with meat stock, however.) Azerbaijanis make good use of dried fruit and nuts, so pilafs are usually more than just seasoned rice. There are also many meatless appetizers that can be combined to make a full meal.

Azeri is the national tongue. Russian can be helpful. Armenian (p. 116) is spoken by a small minority of the population.

Azeri

I would like something without ____.	Mən ____ bir shey yemək istərdim.	mahn ____ beer shay yeh-MAHK ee-stahr-deem.
meat	ətsiz	aht-SEEZ
chicken	toyugsuz	toy-oo**kh**-SOOZ
fish	balygsyz	bah-lih**kh**-SIHZ
eggs	yumurtasyz	yoo-moor-tah-SIHZ
cheese ____	pendirsiz	pehn-deer-SIHZmahn
I do not eat ____.	Mən ____ yemirəm.	mahn ____ yeh-MEER-ahm.
I eat ____ and ____.	Mən ____ və ____ yeyirəm.	mahn ____ vah ____ yeh-YEER-ahm
meat	ət	aht
chicken	toyugət	toy-oog-aht
fish	balyg	bah-lihg
eggs	yumurta	yoo-moor-TAH
cheese	pendir	pehn-DEER
Please	Buyurun	boy-yoo-roon
Thank you	Chokh sag olun	choh**kh** sah**kh** oh-LOON

Bahrain

Bahrain offers the standard cuisine of the Gulf region—which is to say it offers little in the way of culinary enticement to vegetarians. Rice and meat form the centerpiece of the Bahraini diet, but Lebanese-style food such as *falafel* is fairly common. The presence of many foreign workers in Bahrain ensures that there is a fair selection of Asian cuisine: Indian, Pakistani, Thai, Filipino, and Chinese restaurants are present. As a final option, Western-style restaurants or hotel restaurants usually can rustle up a meatless dish.

Arabic (p. 110) is the main language. Other West Asian languages such as Farsi (p. 121) and Urdu (Hindi—p. 180) are spoken by foreign workers. English is a common second language.

Cyprus

Cyprus is currently riven into two parts. The northern half is occupied by Turkish troops and considers itself an independent country. (Most of the rest of the world disagrees.) The southern half of the island is mainly inhabited by ethnic Greeks. As a result of this sharp division, travelers will find that food in the north is much like food in Turkey, while food in the unoccupied zone strongly resembles Greek food in many ways. Still, the foods of the two regions share more similarities than zealots on either side care to admit. Due to its geographical location, there is also a strong Middle Eastern influence throughout the island. (Pita bread and *hummus* are widely available, for example.)

Although Cypriots enjoy meat and fish, it is perfectly possible for vegetarians to eat well in Cyprus. During Lent, Eastern Orthodox Cypriots avoid meat, fish, and dairy products, and many dishes are designed to be served at this time. The rest of the year, *tavernas* offer a wide selection of *meze* (appetizers), many of which are flesh-free. There is also an excellent variety of meatless soups and main dishes, which may contain beans or lentils, cracked wheat, yogurt, eggplant (aubergine), greens, or rice.

Cyprus is linguistically split along the same lines as its political and gastronomic divisions. Most people in northern Cyprus speak **Turkish** (p. 127); the more numerous southern Cypriots speak **Greek** (p. 69). Cyprus was formerly administered by Britain, so English is also widely spoken as a second language.

Georgia

Many Georgians look down on vegetarianism as something of an effete and undesirable habit. Nonetheless, while vegetarianism *per se* is not practiced widely in Georgia, the country has an astounding variety of meatless dishes. Many of these dishes were developed to cope with the lengthy meatless religious fasts of the Georgian Orthodox church, but they are usually available throughout the year. Eggplant (aubergine) is one of the most common dishes, and is served in many forms. *Lobio* (bean-based dishes) are also easily available, but are sometimes made with meat stock. Grains or vegetables are usually served with a sauce; sauces sometimes contain meat, but are often made with garlic, herbs, yogurt, or nuts (especially walnuts). *Khachapuri* (bread filled with cheese) is a common snack. Georgia's fertile soil and good climate ensure that vegetables, fruit, and nuts are widely available and widely used (fruit is dried for use throughout the year). Dairy products are also very common; most cheese is made from sheep or goat milk, and Georgian yogurt is outstanding (and its consumption is widely believed to be the reason for the longevity of the centenarians who inhabit the mountains).

   Georgian (not the drawl heard in Atlanta) is the official language. Russian (p. 100) and Armenian (p. 116) are spoken by small minorities.

Georgian

The words below have been transliterated from Georgian script.

I would like something without ____.	Tu sheydzleba, rame ____.	too SHAYDS-lay-bah, RAH-may ____.
meat	u xortsod	oo **KHOHRT**-sohd
chicken	katmis xortsis gareshe	kaht-mees **KHOHRT**-sees GAH-ray-shay
fish	utevzod	OO-tehv-zohd
eggs	kvertsxis gareshe	kvehr-**EHTS**-**kh**ees

cheese	uxvelod	OO**KH**-vay-lohd
I do not eat _____.	Arvcham ____.	AHRV-chahm ____.
I eat _____ and _____.	Meh vcham ____ da ____.	mayv chahm ____ dah ____.
meat	xorts	**kh**ohrts
chicken	katmis xorts	kaht-mees **kh**ohrts
fish	tevz	tayvz
eggs	kvertsks	k**VAYRTS**ks
cheese	kvels	kvayls
Thank you	Madlobt	MAHD-lohbt

Iran

Visitors who are allowed into the country will find that the basic staple is rice, served either plain or mixed with fruit, meat, or vegetables. Rice pilaf is a common dish, but it is usually made with meat stock. Salads are generally available, but otherwise apart from rice dishes the order of the day is *kebabs*—not good news for vegetarians. There are some interesting meatless Iranian soups, such as yogurt or fruit soups, but these can be difficult to find. Near the Gulf and along the Caspian Sea, pesco-vegetarians will find plenty of fish. There are a few Western-style or Indian restaurants in the cities (although the number of the former has understandably decreased since the Islamic Revolution).

Farsi (Persian) is the predominant language, and is spoken in various dialects. Farsi-derived Dari (p. 190) and Tajik (p. 194) are used in the northeast. Kurdish (p. 122) is spoken in the far northwest. Turkic languages such as Azeri (p. 117) and Turkmen (p. 195) are spoken in some parts of the far north and east. The words and phrases below have been transliterated from the Persian alphabet.

Farsi (Persian)

I would like something without _____.	Man yek chizy bedane _____ mikhaham.	mahn yehk CHEE-zee beh-doh-nay _____ mee-**KH**AH-hahm.
I do not eat _____.	Man _____ nemikhoram.	mahn _____ nay-mee-**kh**oh-rahm.
I eat _____ and _____.	Man _____ va _____ mikhoram.	mahn _____ vah _____ mee-**kh**oh-rahm.
meat	gosht	goosht
chicken	morgh	mohrk
fish	mahi	mah-hee
eggs	tohkme-morgh	to**kh**-may-mohrk
cheese	paneer	pah-NEER
I am a vegetarian.	Man sabzeekar hastam.	mahn sab-zee-kahr hah-STAHM
Please	Lotfan	loht-FAHN
Thank you	Mersy	mehrr-SEE
or	Mamnoon	mahm-NOON

Iraq

Iraqi food is not particularly distinguished. Traditionally, meat has been a major ingredient in Iraqi cooking, although the United Nations embargo cut into its dominance by making meat quite expensive. Many meatless foods of Lebanese origin, such as *falafel*, *hummus*, *tabouli*, and *baba ghanoush*, are on offer. These are generally served with thin Iraqi-style pita bread or French bread, and are the most accessible and widely available meatless options.

Rice dishes are common, but these are often cooked in meat stock. Assorted vegetable or legume soups and stews make appearances, but again, these often contain meat stock or bits of meat. Iraqi-style pizza is also available.

Arabic (p. 110) is the official language. **Kurdish** is spoken in the north.

Kurdish

I do not eat _____.	Ez ____ na xwem.	ahz ____ nah **khw**ahm.
I eat _____ **and _____.**	Ez ____ û ____ dixwem.	ahz ____ oouh ____ teh-**KHW**AHM.
meat	gosht	goosht
chicken	mirishk	meh-REHSHK
fish	masi	mah-seh
eggs	heq	hahk
cheese	penir	pah-NEHR
Please	Lotfen	loht-FAHN
Thank you	Spas	spahz

Israel and Palestine

Vegetarians will find it reasonably easy to find suitable sustenance in Israel and Palestine. There are a number of specialty vegetarian restaurants in Israel, although it is rarely necessary to resort to them. Lacto-vegetarians will be pleased at the number of dairy restaurants in Israel; orthodox Judaism forbids the consumption of milk and meat at the same time, and this proscription has led to a proliferation of Kosher dairy restaurants that serve no meat or fish at all. Ordinary restaurants often offer meatless dishes, especially salads and prepared vegetables such as eggplant (aubergine). Many soups are made with meat stock, however. Because Israel has seen so much immigration, cuisines from all over the world are represented, and provide an interesting change of pace.

The most popular fast food throughout Israel and Palestine is *falafel*, which is sold at stands, shops, and restaurants everywhere. It is served in pita bread, often covered in *tahini* (sesame paste). Roasted corn-on-the-cob (maize) and *bourekas*, flaky pastries with a (usually) meatless cheese or vegetable filling, are also common snacks. Those who cook for themselves will find a wonderful variety of fruits and vegetables available, as well as good yogurt and other dairy products. The word *pareve* on packaging means that the food was prepared without milk or meat.

The food in Palestinian areas does not differ dramatically from that in Israel itself, although Kosher restaurants are understandably absent. *Hummus*, *falafel*, and *fuul* (kidney or fava beans) are popular, and many common *mazza* (appetizers) are meatless. Spinach pastries are filling, cheap, and ubiquitous.

Hebrew and **Arabic** (p. 110) are the official languages of Israel. Hebrew is the predominant tongue in Israel proper; Arabic is the main language in Palestinian areas of Gaza and the West Bank. English is widely spoken in Israel.

Hebrew

Hebrew has its own alphabet and is read from right to left. In the words and phrases below, Hebrew characters have been transliterated into the Latin alphabet.

I would like something without _____.	Ani avakesh mashehoo bli ____.	ah-NEE ah-vah-KEHSH mah-sheh-HOO blee ____.
We would like something without _____.	Anachnu nevakesh mashehoo bli ____.	ah-NAHKH-noo neh-vah-KEHSH mah-sheh-HOO blee ____.
I do not eat _____. (male speaker)	Ani lo ochel ____.	ah-NEE loh OH-khehl ____.
I do not eat ____. (female speaker)	Ani lo ochelet ____.	ah-NEE loh OH-khehl-eht ____.
I eat _____ and _____.	Ani ochel ____ ve ____.	ah-NEE OH-khehl ____ vay ____.

meat	basar	bah-SAHL
chicken	of	ohff
fish	dag	dahg
eggs	beizim	bay-TZEEM
cheese	gvina	GVEE-nah
I am a vegetarian. (male speaker)	Ani tzimchoni.	ah-NEE tseem-**KHOH**-nee
I am a vegetarian. (female speaker)	Ani tzimchonit.	ah-NEE tseem-**KHOH**-neet
Please	Bevakasha	beh-vah-kah-SHAH
Thank you	Toda	toh-DAH

Jordan

Jordanian food borrows heavily from Lebanese influences. While lamb is a favorite meal, *hummus*, *tabouli*, and the usual suspects are available in abundance. *Falafel* stands are as common in Jordan as hamburger joints are in North America. A Jordanian version of pizza is also fairly common (and very tasty). Several common appetizers and main dishes are meat-free, such as eggplant (aubergine) and rice, various salads, and *fuul* (kidney beans). There are also Western and Asian restaurants in the cities.

Arabic (p. 110) is the official language.

Kuwait

Beware the warm Kuwati welcome: Guests are often greeted with the slaughter of a sheep. As one might imagine from this custom, meatless dishes do not abound in Kuwait. Rice with meat or fish is the rule, sometimes accompanied by vegetables stuffed with meat. *Fuul* (kidney beans) is common, however. The best option for vegetarians in Kuwait (other than to lay low) is probably to take refuge in one of the many Chinese or Indian restaurants. There are a number of American-style fast-food restaurants (with all that that implies for vegetarians). There are also a few Lebanese restaurants that serve *falafel*.

Arabic (p. 110) is the official language.

Lebanon

Most of what is commonly thought of as typical Middle Eastern food—*hummus*, *falafel*, *tabouli*, *baba ghanoush* (eggplant/aubergine dip) and the like—is of Lebanese origin. While lamb, chicken, and fish all make regular appearances in Lebanese kitchens, there are plenty of meatless dishes to choose from, in addition to the stereotypical ones listed above. Lebanon is one of the most fertile countries of the Middle East, and the fruits and vegetables it produces are put to good use in Lebanese dishes. Most produce is fresh and local; eggplant (aubergine), spinach, and other vegetable dishes are commonplace. It is easy to find salads or appetizers served with pita bread and based on grains, greens, or beans such as *fuul* (kidney beans). Lebanese potato salad does not contain eggs.

Arabic (p. 110) and **French** (p. 66) are both official languages. Arabic is more useful, as it is the first language of most Lebanese.

Oman

The typical Omani diet, like the diet of most Gulf countries, is based on rice and fish or lamb (although Omanis tend to spice their food up somewhat more than their neighbors to the north do). However, most restaurants serve some kind of meatless entree; there are even a few vegetarian specialty restaurants (a rarity in the Gulf region). In addition to the many Chinese, Indian, and southeast Asian restaurants, there is a contingent of western-style restaurants whose offerings range from truly uninspiring "international" cuisine to pizza and pasta.

Arabic (p. 110) is the official language.

Qatar

The Qatari diet generally consists of rice with meat or fish. Such a diet obviously holds few attractions for the visiting vegetarian. Fortunately, Indians and Pakistanis make up over one third of Qatar's population. As one would expect, Indian restaurants are common, and are probably the best and most accessible option for meatless dishes (although many of the dishes in these restaurants do contain meat). Western-style restaurants exist, and may be a good option for salads or pasta dishes.

Arabic (p. 110) is the official language. Other West Asian languages and English are also spoken.

Saudi Arabia

Saudi Arabia is the home of a vegetarian's nightmare, the so-called "goat grab," a meal of a whole roast sheep or goat. Such meals are often prepared to welcome visitors, so a vegetarian who is welcomed in this fashion is in a quandary indeed. Apart from these flesh fests, Saudi Arabia can be culinarily manageable. The average Saudi eats lots of rice, although usually with chicken, fish, or lamb. You are free to eat only the rice, although this diet may grow tiresome. *Fuul* (kidney beans) and *samosas* are very common (although the latter often contain meat). Salads and fruit (both fresh and dried) are easy to find. Adventurous non-vegans can try camel milk and cheese. In the cities, Indian, Chinese and other restaurants offer vegetarian dishes. There are also many Western-style restaurants in urban areas, which sometimes serve meatless food such as pizza or pasta. Traveling among the Bedouin of the Saudi desert, you should probably be prepared either to eat meat or go hungry.

Arabic (p. 110) is the principal language. English is often spoken in the cities.

Syria

Syrian food blends influences from Turkey, Lebanon, Armenia, and elsewhere in the Middle East. While meat dishes such as *kebab* or *kibby* (a ground beef mixture) are everywhere, there are plenty of meatless options from which to choose. As in neighboring Lebanon, *hummus, falafel,* and *pita bread* are common offerings. There are many vegetarian side dishes and main dishes, such as eggplant/aubergine (served hot or cold), squash (courgette, marrow, or pumpkin) with yogurt sauce, eggless potato salad, or bean salads. Cracked wheat is often served in salad or in other forms.

Arabic (p. 110) is the official language. Kurdish (p. 122) is spoken in parts of the northeast; Armenian (p. 116) is spoken by a very small minority.

Turkey

Turkish cuisine comprises much more than the stereotypical skewer of shishkebab. In fact, while lamb and other meats are very common and are often served in the form of kebab, there are many options for vegetarians. The most promising dishes are known as *zeytinyagli* (zeh-tin-yah-lee); these are made with olive oil and contain lots of vegetables. *Zeytinyagli* are served cold, usually as *mezze* (appetizers) or side dishes, and are even available in most kebab houses. Be careful in the hinterlands of central and eastern Turkey—cooks may occasionally throw in pieces of meat.

Besides *zeytinyagli*, many side and main dishes are meat-free. Greek-style salads with feta and olives are common; *ali nazik* is an eggplant (aubergine), cheese, and yogurt concoction; *biber dolmasi* contains rice, tomatoes, and spices. *Börek* are savory pastries containing vegetables or cheese (and sometimes meat). Various other dishes are made with a tomato-onion base and contain no meat. However, soups and some cooked bean or vegetable dishes sometimes contain meat stock. Turkish pizza and the bagel-like *simit* make good snacks.

The description above mostly applies to western and, to a lesser extent, central Turkey. In eastern Turkey, entirely vegetarian dishes may be difficult to find; mutton and goat form the basis of the diet and in some cases there may be little else to eat. Pesco-vegetarians should note that fish is served everywhere in coastal regions.

Turkish is the official national language. Kurdish (p. 122) dialects are spoken in the southeast.

Turkish

I would like something without _____.	_____ birsey istiyorum.	_____ beer-SHAY ees-TEE-yoh-room.
We would like something without _____.	_____ birseyler istiyoruz.	_____ beer-shay-LEHR ees-TEE-yoh-rooz.
meat	etsiz	eht-SEEZ
chicken	tavuksuz	tah-vook-SOOZ

fish	balıksız	bah-luhk-SUHZ
eggs	yumurtasız	yoo-moor-tah-SUHZ
cheese	peynirsiz	pay-neer-SEEZ
I do not eat _____.	_____ yemem.	_____ yeh-MAHM.
I eat _____ and _____.	_____ ve _____ yerim.	_____ veh _____ YEH-reem.
meat	et	eht
chicken	tavuk	tah-VOOK
fish	balık	bah-LUHK
eggs	yumurta	yoo-moor-TAH
cheese	peynir	pay-NEER
I am a vegetarian.	Ben vejeteryenim.	behn veh-zheh-tehr-YEHN-eem
Please	Lutfen	LOOT-fahn
Thank you	Tesekkurler	teh-shehk-koor-LEHR

United Arab Emirates

These Emirates are united, among other ways, in their fairly bland diet of rice eaten with meat or fish. However, there are many Western-style restaurants that offer pizza, pasta, salads, and other meatless dishes. Many different Asian cuisines are also represented here; Chinese and Indian/Pakistani restaurants are particularly common. Lebanese-style food (*falafel* and *hummus*) is also available.

Arabic (p. 110) is the official language. Due to the presence of many foreign workers in the U.A.E., many Asian languages, as well as English, are spoken.

Yemen

Yemenis are not heavy meat eaters, but they are hardly intentional vegetarians, either. The standard Yemeni diet consists of grains, bread, or beans, usually served with fish or meat sauce or soup. Most soups have meat or are made with meat stock, but there are some meatless vegetable or yogurt soups that occasionally can be found in local restaurants. A variety of vegetables are eaten as side dishes. *Fuul* (kidney beans) is a common dish, as is *salta* (mixed vegetables with a spicy mustard sauce). Rice is the most common grain, but Yemenis also use potatoes and sorghum. There are a few western-style restaurants serving pasta and the like. As a last resort, one can chew *qat*, a widely used stimulant and appetite suppressant.

Arabic (p. 110) is the main language of Yemen.

Africa South of the Sahara

A frica is a vast continent with substantial regional differences in culture, language, and geography. However, the cuisine of sub-Saharan Africa is not as diverse as that of some other areas of the world, partly because of limited indigenous ingredients and partly because of general poverty.

In most areas of the continent, some kind of starch—rice, (ground maize), millet, or tubers such as yam or cassava—forms the basis of the diet. The starch is generally supplemented by soups, sauces, or stews, which typically contain meat or fish (although they are sometimes vegetable-based). Exact ingredients vary from country to country. The availability of fresh fruit and vegetables also varies wildly. European-style food is common in many urban or resort areas, although all too often it is the worst of neo-colonial cuisine: greasy french fries, steak or hamburger, or some other unhealthy concoction. Indian or Middle Eastern food can be found in some countries.

Throughout most of sub-Saharan Africa, cheese is not an indigenous food, but imported cheese may be available. In these areas the word from the relevant colonial language is used to mean cheese (e.g., *fromage* in former French colonies).

Thousands of languages are spoken in Africa, most of which are very limited in geographical range. The prevalence of minor tribal languages, combined with the arbitrary nature of post-colonial boundaries, means that most African countries have no universally spoken indigenous language. (Conversely, some African languages are spoken in more than one country.) The official language of most countries is the European language of the relevant former colonial power. In many countries, not everyone can speak the official language, but people who are used to dealing with tourists or who have received formal education usually can. In some countries, an indigenous language has become the *de facto* tongue of inter-ethnic communication.

The most useful regional languages are Hausa (p. 140), Bambara-Dioula (p. 138), and Wolof (p. 144) in West Africa; Swahili (p. 151) in East Africa; and Afrikaans (p. 170) in parts of southern Africa.

A. WEST AFRICA

While the quality of West African food varies from one country to another, the basic substance is the same throughout much of the region. The standard meal is starch with sauce or soup, sometimes accompanied by vegetables and greens. The starch is usually rice, millet, or some form of cassava, banana, yam, or sweet potato. The sauces are often marvelous, frequently based on vegetables or peanuts. However, even vegetable or nut sauces sometimes contain meat or fish; fish is the most common additive along the coast or near major rivers, while chicken or lamb are used in inland areas. Okra and other vegetables, or greens such as cassava leaves, are served as side dishes. Western-style food is available in some countries, and is usually most prevalent in urban areas.

Benin

Beninese food fits the standard West African model: starch (usually rice, cassava, or yam) with sauce or stew. Sauces in Benin tend to display more flair than those in some other countries in the region. Unfortunately, these sauces usually contain meat, although there are a few purely vegetarian sauces, typically based on okra or spinach-like greens. Meatless peanut sauce is sometimes available. Pesco-vegetarians will be happy to know that fish is available everywhere along the coast, and along rivers in inland areas; sardines with tomatoes is a common dish. Cotonou has a few European-style restaurants that serve pizza, pasta, French bread, and other accoutrements of neo-colonialism.

French (p. 66) is the official language. In the south, Yoruba (p. 142) is common. Various tribal languages are spoken in the north.

Burkina Faso

Burkina Faso is a fascinating but poor country with an equally poor selection of vegetarian food. Most restaurants, such as they are, concentrate on grilled meat or fish and are neither particularly representative of Burkinan food nor very amenable to vegetarianism. Food stalls are a better (if less sanitary) bet for vegetarians. The core of the diet of most "Burkinabae" is millet or rice with sauce. Most homemade sauces are vegetarian (due to the cost of meat), but stall-bought sauces are likely to contain some meat. Stews such as yam stew and okra stew are common, as are plain greens and sweet potatoes. European-style restaurants, bakeries, and creameries in Ouagadougou and Bobo Dioulasso provide a break from food stall fare.

French (p. 66) is the official language. The main market language is Dioula-Bambara (p. 138). Many other indigenous languages are spoken, including Hausa (p. 140) and Pulaar (p. 139).

Cape Verde

The Cape Verde archipelago is bathed in the waters of the tropical Atlantic, so it should come as no shock that fish is the mainstay of the diet. Pesco-vegetarians should have a field day, but strict vegetarians will run into problems. Rice is the staple starch, and it's sometimes eaten with beans; fried banana is a typical side dish. Turnovers and other pastry-type dishes are common snacks, but they often contain fish or meat.

Portuguese (p. 73) is the official language, and is widely spoken. The main everyday language is Crioulo, a mixture of Portuguese and African dialects.

Crioulo

I do not eat _____.	Um ka pode come ____.	oom kah pohd koh-may ____.
meat	carne	kahrn
chicken	galinha	gah-leen-yah
fish	peixe	paysh
eggs	of	ohf
Thank you (female speaker)	Obrigada	oh-bree-GAH-dah
Thank you (male speaker)	Obrigado	oh-bree-GAH-doh

Côte d'Ivoire (Ivory Coast)

Ivoirien cuisine tends to follow the starch-and-sauce model of other West African countries. The starches include *foutou* (pounded, pasta-like starchy cakes) made from cassava, yam, plantain, or banana, rice, or *attieke* (grated cassava) made into a sort of couscous. Generally, the starches are served with sauces made with chicken, fish, or occasionally beef, but it is sometimes possible to get vegetable sauces. Food stalls often sell snacks such as bananas or plantains, grilled and mashed or fried in palm oil. The cities of Côte d'Ivoire host more European restaurants than most other West African countries do, and French, Italian, and other cuisines are available. There are a few Chinese and Middle Eastern restaurants in Abidjan.

French (p. 66) is the official language. Of the 60-plus native dialects, Bambara-Dioula (p. 138) is the most common, and is used as a market language everywhere.

The Gambia

The Gambia is a long, skinny country strung along the river of the same name that is the lifeblood of the country, and fish is correspondingly important in the Gambian diet. Rice, millet, and mashed cassava or yam are all widely used starches. These are usually served with stews that are sometimes vegetarian, but are often made with fish or chicken. (For example, peanut stew is common, but frequently contains chicken.) Restaurants tend to concentrate on chicken and fish dishes. French fries and other unhealthy Western snack foods are easily available.

English is the official language; several indigenous languages are spoken in The Gambia. Wolof (p. 144) is the most common indigenous language along the coast. In the interior, there are speakers of Dioula-Bambara (p. 138), Pulaar (p. 139), and **Mandinka**, as well as several other tongues.

Mandinka

I do not eat _____.	Mbu ka _____ domo.	mBOO kah ___ doh-moh.
meat	subo	soo-boh
chicken	sousse	soo-say

fish	ñie	nyeh
eggs	sousse kilo	soo-say kee-loh
Thank you	Abaraka	ah-bah-RAH-kah

Ghana

Along with the standard West African starches—rice, cassava, millet, yam, plantain, and corn (maize)—Ghanians turn out some wonderful sauces. Sadly, most of these sauces, including peanut sauce, are usually made with chicken or fish. With some diligent searching (or a pleasant manner), it is often possible to find vegetable sauces or stews made with pumpkin or other squashes, spinach, okra, or eggplant (aubergine). Fried sweet potato is a common snack food, as are (ground maize) balls and fried plantains. In Accra and to a lesser extent in cities throughout the country, Western-style food is reasonably common, but not necessarily helpful to vegetarians. (For example, fish and chips is popular, reflecting Ghana's British colonial history.) There are a few Indian, Middle Eastern, and assorted other seemingly misplaced eateries in the cities.

English is the official language. Nearly half the population speaks **Twi**. Some Hausa (p. 140) is spoken in the north, while Ewe (p. 145) is spoken in the southeast.

Twi

I do not eat _____.	Mi ndi ____.	meen-DEE ____.
meat (this word also encompasses fish)	nam	nahm
chicken	akoko	ah-koh-koh
eggs	kosier	KOH-see-ehrr
Thank you	Medasi	may-DAH-see

Guinea

In common with its neighbors, rice or other starches with sauce is the standard Guinean meal. Usually the sauce contains fish or occasionally chicken, but vegetarian varieties are sometimes available. Fried bananas are a common snack, and other fruits such as pineapple are common. There are a few Western restaurants in Conakry, including some French cafes; outside Conakry, there is very little variation in available food.

French (p. 66) is the official language. Many indigenous languages are spoken in the interior, including Pulaar (p. 139).

Guinea-Bissau

The cuisine of Guinea-Bissau is not particularly distinguished. Fish is a staple, and rice, yam, and cassava are the usual starches. Fried bananas are a common snack. There are Western-style restaurants in the capital, which may be good sources for welcome, if unimaginative, meatless food.

Portuguese (p. 73) is the official language. The lingua franca is **Crioulo** (p. 134). Wolof (p. 144), Mandinka (p. 135) and other indigenous languages are also spoken.

Liberia

Liberia's unfortunate recent history of civil war and famine means that there is very little variety to the average Liberian's diet. Cassava, rice, and sweet potatoes are the most common starches. These are traditionally topped with a sauce or stew, and served with greens such as cassava leaves or okra. With luck, the sauce will be vegetarian—meat is difficult to come by during times of privation and dislocation. If peace can be maintained, it is likely that a greater variety of food will become available to both the local population and the traveler.

English is the official language, and the small minority of Liberians who are of African-American descent speak it as a mother tongue. More than two dozen local languages are spoken in Liberia.

Mali

Mali is a dry, dusty (albeit historically fascinating) country with relatively little variety in its cuisine. "Couscous" (made from millet) and rice are the staple starches. Soups, stews, and sauces usually are served with the starches. Unfortunately, sauces almost always contain meat, typically chicken (or lamb in the north). Grilled meat is popular in cities. Vegetables and fruit are fairly uncommon but can be found seasonally. Pesco-vegetarians will find that fish is available along the rivers. Bamako has a few European-style establishments that serve vegetable side dishes, pasta, and other welcome variations on the starch-sauce-meat theme.

French (p. 66) is the official language. **Bambara** is the most widely spoken indigenous language; in other West African countries, it is known as **Dioula**. Arabic (p. 110) is used in some regions. Hausa (p. 140) is spoken by some people in the eastern part of the country, and Pulaar (p. 139) is fairly common, especially in the north and west.

Bambara-Dioula

I would like something without ____.	Ne be ____tan doumounidofe.	nay bay ____TAHN doo-moh-nee-DOH-fay.
I do not eat ____.	Ne te ____ doun.	nay tay ____ doon.
I eat ____.	Ne be ____lou du.	nay nay ____LOO doo.
meat	sogo	soh-goh
chicken	che	shay
fish	jege	jay-gay
eggs	chéfam	shay-FAHM
Thank you	Iniche	EE-nee-shay

Mauritania

Mauritania is not a very vegetarian-friendly destination. Very few fruits or vegetables (other than dates) are available outside of cities. The focus of most meals is meat such as lamb or camel, generally served with rice, millet "couscous," or occasionally pasta. The northern part of the country is especially bleak territory for vegetarians. There is more variety in the south, where some Senegalese influence creeps in. Nouakchott has several European restaurants serving pasta, pizza, or other such dainties. Pesco-vegetarians can find fish along the coast or in areas bordering the Senegal River.

The Hasaniya dialect of **Arabic** (p. 110) is official. French (p. 66), formerly the official language, is still widely used in business and government. **Wolof** (p. 144) is also an official language, and is spoken throughout much of the southern part of the country. Several other African languages are spoken, including **Pulaar**, the language of a semi-nomadic people of the Sahel.

Pulaar

I would like something without _____.	Mido yidi ko alaa _____.	MEE-doh YEE-dee koh ah-LAH _____.
I do not eat _____.	Mi ñaamataa _____.	mee nyah-mah-tah _____.
I eat _____ and _____.	Mido ñaama _____ e _____.	MEE-doh nyah-mah _____ ay _____.
meat	teewu	tay-oo
chicken	ndiwri	ndee-wree
fish	liddi	lee-dee
eggs	boccoode	boh-choh-day
I am a vegetarian. (literally, "I do not eat living things")	Mi ñaamataa ko wadi fittaandu.	mee nyah-mah-tah koh wah-DEE FIH-tahn-doo
Thank you	A jaaraama	AH jahr-ah-mah

Niger

Restaurants in Niger tend to emphasize meat or fish on their menus. If you wish to avoid these items, you had better like millet, which is the main staple food throughout most of the country. Sorghum is also a common ingredient. Millet is served with sauces that may or may not contain meat; spicy tomato sauce or peanut sauce is a common topping and is often meat-free. Millet and bean cakes with spicy powder and *meringa olifera* leaf balls with onion are common snacks. The daring may wish to try Niger's unique hard goat, sheep, or camel cheese (which may be highly unsanitary if uncooked). In the north, rice is the staple grain, and is usually served with lamb. Fish-eaters should gravitate towards the banks of the Niger River, where fish is served with particular frequency.

French (p. 66) is the official language. **Hausa** is spoken in the southern part of the country, while **Zarma** is spoken in the west. Pulaar (p. 139) is spoken by some of the nomadic tribes of the north.

Hausa

I would like something without _____.	Ina son wane abu wanda baya da _____.	EE-nah sohn WAH-nay AH-boo WAHN-dah BYE-ah dah _____.
We would like something without _____.	Muna son wane abu wanda baya da _____.	MOO-nah sohn WAH-nay AH-boo WAHN-dah BYE-ah dah _____.
I do not eat _____. but it is better to say (literally, "I am not used to")	Ba ni chi _____. Ban saba ba _____.	bah nee chee _____. bahn SAH-bah bah _____.
I eat _____ and _____.	Ina chi _____ da _____.	EE-nah chee _____ dah _____.
meat	nama	NAH-mah
chicken	kaza	kah-ZAH

fish	kihi	kee-hee
eggs	kwe	kway
Thank you	Na gode	nah GOH-day

Zarma

I would like something without _____.	Ay ga ba hayfo kan sinda _____.	eye gah BAH hye-FOH kahn SEEN-dah _____.
We would like something without _____.	Ir ga ba hayfo kan sinda _____.	eer gah BAH hye-FOH kahn SEEN-dah _____.
I do not eat _____.	Ay si nwa _____.	eye seeg nah _____.
I eat _____ and _____.	Ay ga nwa _____ da _____.	eye gah VAH _____ jah _____.
meat	ham	hahm
chicken	gorno	GOHR-noh
fish	hamisa	hah-MEE-sah
eggs	gouri	goo-REE
Thank you	Ay sa bo	eye sah boo
or	Fofo	foh-foh

Nigeria

Most Nigerians love meat but cannot afford to eat it on a regular basis. This means that restaurants almost always concentrate on meat: The logic is if someone is spending money on a meal out, they must want flesh in their food. Similarly, as an honored guest in a home, it may be difficult to gratefully refuse to eat meat that has been prepared for you. Vegetarianism is not really understood in Nigeria, but it is sometimes accepted as one of those strange things foreigners do. Food stalls and takeaways are better bets for meatless dishes. The staple starches are pounded yam, cassava, and *gari* (fermented cassava meal); the starch is usually dipped in a soup or sauce based on peanuts, beans, or greens such as okra, spinach, or melon seed. Meat or fish is usually tossed in for people who can afford it. (Because foreign travelers invariably look like they can afford it, it is better to strike preemptively and ask that meat be left out.) Snack food such as bean cakes or french fries, although not especially healthy, are a good option because they usually contain no meat.

English is the official language, but there are over 400 indigenous languages spoken in Nigeria. The most common of these is **Yoruba**, which is spoken by more than a quarter of Nigerians, mainly in the southwest. **Ibo** is spoken in the southwest and in the Niger Delta area. Hausa (p. 140) is spoken by a large chunk of the population, mainly in the north and northwest.

Yoruba

I do not eat _____.	Iyi jẹ _____.	ee-yee jeh _____.
I eat _____.	Moman jẹ _____.	moh-mahn jeh _____.
meat	ẹran	eh-rahn
chicken	ẹran ẹdirẹ	eh-rahn eh-dee-ray
fish	ẹja	eh-jah
eggs	ẹyin	eh-yeen
Thank you	Oṣehoun	OH-shay-hoon

Ibo

I do not eat _____.	A n'ahum eri _____.	ah NAH-hoom ay-ree _____.
I eat _____ and _____.	A n'am eri _____ n' _____.	ah NAHM ay-ree _____ nah _____.
meat	anu	AH-noo
chicken	anu okuko	AH-noo oh-kuh-koh
fish	azu	AAZ-oo
eggs	akwa	aak-WAH
Thank you	Ndaewo	nDAY-woh
or	Daalu	DAH-loo

Senegal

Senegalese cuisine is often regarded as the best and most creative in West Africa. Unfortunately, Senegal is no more vegetarian-friendly than its neighbors. Rice or millet with sauce or soup is the basic pattern; usually, as alluring as it may be in other respects, the sauce or soup contains meat or fish. Vegetables are often served as side dishes, but there are relatively few vegetarian main dishes. One exception is vegetable *mafé* served with rice and porridge. Rice and vegetables in tomato sauce can sometimes be found. Senegal's celebrated peanut sauce is typically made with chicken, although meatless versions can sometimes be found. Pesco-vegetarians should have no trouble in Senegal; the national dish is *tiebou djenn* (fish and vegetable stew), and fish in other forms is very common. In Dakar and large towns there are French restaurants and cafes and other European-style eateries that sometimes serve vegetarian entrees.

French (p. 66) is the official language. The most common African language, especially along the coast, is **Wolof**. Other languages such as Pulaar (p. 139), Mandinka (p. 135) and Bambara-Dioula (p. 138) are spoken in inland areas.

Wolof

I would like something without _____.	Dema büg lou amol _____.	DAY-mah buh-GUH loo ah-MOHL _____.
I do not eat _____.	Duma lek _____.	doo-mah lehk _____.
I eat _____ and _____.	Demai lek _____ ack _____.	deh-MYE lehk _____ ahk _____.
meat	yap	yahp
chicken	ginar	GEE-nahr
fish	djenn	jyehn
eggs	nen	nehn
I am a vegetarian. (Literally, "I do not eat living things.")	Duma lek lui dunda.	doo-mah lehk loo-ee DOON-duh
Thank you	Djer jeff	jyehr jehf

Sierra Leone

When the country is not engulfed in civil war, Sierra Leone has surprisingly decent food. As in the rest of the region, rice or tubers such as yams serve as the staple starch, and are served with sauce or soup. The soup is promisingly named by the main vegetable, but usually contains fish or meat. However, there is a small Lebanese population, and (often meatless) Middle Eastern food is sometimes available. There are also a few Indian restaurants in the larger towns. Snacks are often vegetarian; french fries made with white sweet potatoes are frequently available in restaurants and food stalls. Steamed yams, fried plantains, and *fufu* (cassava balls) are all common.

Although **English** is the official language, **Krio** is the lingua franca. Since Krio is derived from English, the average English-speaker should be able to recognize plenty of phrases. Several tribal languages are also spoken.

Krio

I do not eat _____.	Ah no de et ____.	ah noh day eet ____.
meat	mit	meet
chicken	fol	fahl
fish	fish	fish
eggs	eg	ehg
Please	Ah beg	ah behg
Thank you	Thenki	TEHN-kee

Togo

Togolese cuisine is much like the cuisine elsewhere in West Africa: Starches served with sauce are the rule. However, the sauces in Togo tend to be somewhat more refined than in neighboring countries. Along the coast, most sauces contain fish; inland, many sauces are based on vegetables or greens, and meat costs extra. The starch component is likely to be rice or one of several *pâtes* (pasta-like substances) made from cassava, yams, or sometimes vegetables. Millet is common in the drier north. Grilled or fried plantain is a typical street food. Lomé has many European restaurants, and even a few Chinese and Middle Eastern restaurants.

French (p. 66) is the official language. The most common indigenous language is **Ewe**, which is spoken by close to half the population.

Ewe

I would like something without _____.	Medibe madu mu si me ____ me le o.	may-DEE-bay MAH-doo moo see meh ____ meh lay oh.
I do not eat _____.	Nye me du na ____ o.	nyay meh doo nah ____ oh.

I eat _____.	Me du na _____ o.	meh doo nah _____ oh.
meat	lā	lah
chicken	koklolā	koh-kloh-lah
fish	akpavi	ahk-bah-vee
eggs	koklozi	koh-kloh-zee
Thank you	Akpe	ahk-BAY

B. EAST AFRICA

East Africa is something of a culinary mixed bag for vegetarians. In some countries, such as Ethiopia and Eritrea, meatless dishes based on vegetables or legumes are quite easy to find. In other areas, almost everything is served with meat, at least in restaurants and at food stalls, although greens are sometimes available. Pesco-vegetarians should get by with few problems in most of East Africa, particularly near the sea or the Great Lakes. There is a substantial Indian population along the Indian Ocean littoral, and meatless dishes can usually be found at Indian-run restaurants.

Burundi

Burundi, riven by ethnic strife and poverty, does not have what one might call a world-class cuisine. Boiled starches such as corn (maize), cassava, and plantain are the basics of the diet. The starches are usually accompanied by legumes, greens, stews (including peanut stew), and meat or fish. Fish is particularly common near Lake Tanganyika. Bananas and other fruit are relatively easy to find. There were formerly several excellent European restaurants in Bujumbura; very few remain, and they are not particularly interested in vegetarian customers.

French (p. 66) and **Kirundi** are the official languages. Swahili (p. 151) is spoken near the capital and in the eastern part of the country.

Kirundi

I do not eat ____.	Sindya ____.	SEEN-dyah ____.
I eat ____.	Ndadya ____.	nDAH-dyah ____.
meat	inyama	een-yah-mah
chicken	inkoko	ihn-HOH-koh
fish	ifi	ee-fee
eggs	amagi	ah-mah-gee
Thank you	Urakoze	oo-rah-KOH-zeh

Djibouti

The staple food of Djibouti is rice with fish or meat. It is also easy to find *lahooh* (a flat wheat bread similar to the *injera* of Ethiopia), which is often served with a sauce or soup made of vegetables or pulses such as lentils. Spaghetti is reasonably common, although it is usually served with meat sauce. There are some Indian restaurants, and these may be the best options for vegetarian dishes. There is also a selection of French-style cafes and restaurants.

French (p. 66) and **Arabic** (p. 110) are both official languages. Somali (p. 153) is spoken by a large proportion of the population.

Eritrea

Eritrea is a fairly easy country in which to be a vegetarian. Much of the population abstains from meat two days a week throughout the year, and for weeks at a time during Lent and the pre-Christmas period. Many grain and legume dishes (such as unleavened bread with spicy lentils) have been developed to deal with the meatless fasts; while these are obviously most easily available on fasting days, they can be found in some restaurants on any day of the week. Greens, assorted vegetables, and fruit are all common, although the arid climate limits the variety of fresh local produce. As a result of Eritrea's long occupation by Italy, spaghetti and other kinds of pasta are popular, although they are often served with meat sauces.

Tigrinya is the main indigenous language. Because the country was a province of Ethiopia for decades, many Eritreans can speak Amharic. Arabic is also useful. Some older people can speak Italian. Secondary education is now conducted in English, so the usefulness of English is likely to increase. English, Tigrinya, and Arabic are the main working languages of the government.

Tigrinya

Tigrinya uses its own writing system. The words and phrases below have been transliterated into the Roman alphabet.

| **I would like something without _____.** | Zkone megbi bzey _____. | zuh-KOH-neh MEHG-bee bih-zay _____. |

I do not eat _____.	Ane ayblen _____ eyé.	ah-nay ay-beh-leh-ehn _____ EYE-eh.
meat	sga	sih-gah
chicken	derho	dohr-hoh
fish	asa	ah-SAH
eggs	enquaquho	ehn-kwah-koo-hoh
I eat _____ **and** _____.	Ane _____ _____ yibele.	ah-nay _____ _____ yih-beh-LEH.
meat	sgan	sih-gahn
chicken	derhon	dohr-hohn
fish	asan	ah-sahm
eggs	enquaquhon	ehn-kwah-koo-hohn
Please (female speaker)	Bejaki	beh-jah-KEE
Please (male speaker)	Bejaka	beh-jah-KAH
Thank you	Yekenyeley	yeh-kehn-YEH-lye

Ethiopia

Although few Ethiopians are actually vegetarians, there are plenty of meat-free dishes available around the country. (The relative abundance of vegetarian food is partly a result of the frequent meatless fasts undertaken by Ethiopian Orthodox Christians.) The base for most meals is *injera*, a spongy, unleavened bread made with teff, wheat or sorghum. The *injera* is usually covered by or served with some sort of sauce or *wat* (stew). Typically, the sauce will contain meat or fish, but vegetable stew, lentil stew, and spiced vegetables are all common meatless alternatives. Greens and sometimes even cottage cheese are also occasionally available. There are some Western restaurants in Addis Ababa and other large cities; pasta is usually on offer at these establishments.

The official language of Ethiopia is **Amharic**. Tigrinya (p. 148) and several other indigenous languages are spoken in the provinces. Somali (p. 153) and Arabic (p. 110) are spoken in parts of northern Ethiopia. Italian and English are the most commonly spoken European languages.

Amharic

Amharic is written in a lovely but difficult-to-reproduce script. The following phrases have been transliterated into the Roman alphabet.

I would like something without ____.	____ yelelebet mighib efelgalehu.	____ yeh-LEH-leh-beht mee-geeb eh-fehl-GAH-loo.
We would like something without ____.	____ yelelebet mighib enfelegalen.	____ yeh-LEH-leh-beht mee-geeb ehn-feh-leh-gah-LEHN.
I do not eat ____.	____ albelam.	____ ahl-beh-LAHM.
I eat ____ and ____.	____ ena ____ ebelalehu.	____ EH-nah ____ eh-beh-lah-LEH-hoo.
meat	siga	sih-gah
chicken	doro	doh-roh
fish	assa	ah-sah
eggs	inqulal	ihn-koo-LAHL
cheese	ayeb	eybh
Please	Ebako	eh-bah-KOH
Thank you	Ameseghinalehu	ah-meh-seh-GEH-nah-loo

Kenya

The national dish of Kenya is *ugali* (cornmeal/ground-maize or millet porridge), potatoes, or rice served with stew. This combination can be found all over the country, but unfortunately the stew usually contains meat. (Even vegetable stews are generally made with stock or gravy.) Vegetarians can sometimes supplement the starches with greens such as spinach, or occasionally with beans; fruit and fruit juice are widely available. Many Kenyans are of Indian descent and Indian restaurants are found in cities throughout the country. Indian restaurants almost always serve some vegetarian food, and they are especially common in Mombasa and elsewhere along the coast. Nairobi and Mombasa have quite a few Western-style restaurants that serve the usual suspects, including pasta. Many Kenyan game lodges offer vegetarian entrees, although sometimes veggie dishes must be requested in advance.

Although few people speak it as a native tongue except along the coast, **Swahili** is the *lingua franca* of Kenya and much of the rest of East Africa. Most Kenyans speak one of several tribal languages as their first language. **English** is also an official language.

Swahili

I would like something without ____.	Tafadhali ninitaka chakula bila ____.	tah-fah-DAH-lee nee-nee-TAH-kah shah-KOO-lah bee-lah ____.
We would like something without ____.	Tafadhali tunaktaka chakula bila ____.	tah-fah-DAH-lee too-nahk-TAH-kah shah-KOO-lah bee-lah ____.
I do not eat ____.	Sikuli ____.	see-koo-lee ____.
I eat ____ and ____.	Kula ____ na ____.	koo-lah ____ nah ____.
meat	nyama	nyah-mah
chicken	kuku	koo-koo
fish	samaki	sah-mah-kee

eggs	mayai	mah-yah-ee
Please	Tafadhali	tah-fah-DAH-lee
Thank you	Asante	ah-sahn-tay

Rwanda

Starches and legumes are the order of the day in Rwanda. Cassava or corn (maize) with beans and plantain or banana with split peas or beans is the typical meal. Rwandans who can afford it invariably add meat or fish, so most eateries do not concentrate on vegetarian dishes. Some greens and vegetables can be found, and bananas are ubiquitous. Tea and coffee are the main crops, but you are unlikely to find them a satisfying option for long-term sustenance. There are very few Western restaurants left in the country.

French (p. 66) is one official language; the other is **Kinyarwanda**, which is essentially the same language as **Kirundi** (p. 147). Swahili (p. 151) is also useful in many parts of the country.

Seychelles

The food of the Seychelles is a mixture of European, Indian, Chinese, and semi-indigenous Creole cuisine. Creole food is typically fish, pork, or chicken served with herbed rice; there is a disturbing tendency to use fruit bat in stews and curries. Vegetables such as calabash, eggplant (aubergine), golden apple, red peppers (capsicum), and choux choux are used in some dishes. Tropical fruit is reasonably common, and fried or boiled bananas, sometimes made with coconut milk, are frequently served as a side dish. Starches such as cassava, sweet potato, and breadfruit are also typical ingredients. Apart from Creole cooking (which is not always easily found in restaurants), there are Indian and Chinese restaurants on several islands and throughout Victoria; Indian restaurants almost invariably serve vegetarian dishes. Hotel restaurants and other eateries catering to tourists tend to concentrate on European or "international" cuisine, with no particular emphasis on meatless food. Pasta is quite common, however.

French (p. 66) and **English** are the official languages, but French-derived Seychelles **Creole** is the first language of most islanders.

Creole

I do not eat _____.	Mon pa manz ____.	mawn pah mahnz ____.
meat	la vyan	lah vee-ahn
chicken	le poul	luh pool
fish	le pwason	luh pwah-zahn
eggs	dizef	dee-zehff
Thank you	Merci	mehr-see

Somalia

Somalis have traditionally been nomadic herders, and thus milk and meat are important parts of the diet. (Constant factional warfare does not encourage rapid adoption of settled agriculture.) Very few vegetables are consumed, although mangoes and bananas are grown locally, and vegetable curries can sometimes be found. *Injira*, Ethiopian-style unleavened bread, is a common food, but is usually covered with meat sauce. Rice and spaghetti (a legacy of Italian rule) are also frequently eaten, but are typically served with meat sauce. Some towns have Indian or Middle Eastern eateries, which are the best choices for vegetarians.

Somali, a language derived from Arabic, is the national tongue. Swahili (p. 151) may be useful in the far south. Italian is potentially useful in the southern half of the country.

Somali

There are northern and southern dialects in Somali. The phrases and words below are in the northern dialect, but they should still be understood in other regions of the country. The phrases below have been transliterated into the Roman alphabet from Somali Arabic script.

I would like something without _____.	Waxaan doonayaa cunto aan ____ lahayn.	wah-**KHAHN** doo-nah-**YAH** NN-toh ahn ____ lah-hyne.

We would like something without _____.	Waxaan soonaynaa cunto aan _____ lahayn.	wah-**KH**AHN doo-nye-NAH NN-toh ahn _____ lah-hyne.
I do not eat _____.	Ma aan cuno _____.	mah-ahn NN-oh _____.
I eat _____ and _____.	Waxaan cunaa _____ iyo _____.	wah **KH**AHN nn-AH _____ ee-yoh _____.
meat	hilib	hih-lihbb
chicken	digaag	dih-GAHG
fish	kaluun	kah-LUHN
eggs	ukun	uh-kuhn
Please	Walaal	wah-LAHL
Thank you	Mahadsamid	mah-hahd-sah-meed

Sudan

Sudan is divided into two cultural and culinary worlds. The south of Sudan is culturally distinct from the rest of the country, and the food there (often in short supply because of an ongoing civil war) is fairly typical of sub-Saharan Africa: Millet, starches, stews, sauces, and greens are the norm. In northern Sudan, the food is much like that of Egypt and parts of the Middle East; *fuul* (kidney beans) with pita bread, lentil dishes, and soups and stews (sometimes vegetarian) are common dishes. Somewhat more variety is available in Khartoum, which features a number of restaurants and cafes serving European or Middle Eastern cuisine.

Arabic (p. 110) is the official language and is spoken predominantly in the north. Indigenous African languages are spoken in the south of the country, and by refugees from the south. An aggressive policy of Arabicization is increasing the use of Arabic in southern regions.

Tanzania

Starches (especially corn/maize) and beans are the mainstays of the Tanzanian diet. Stews are common accompaniments, but meat or fish is added whenever possible. Fish is particularly common along the coast and near lakes Victoria and Tanganyika. There are some standard meatless dishes based on peanuts, greens, pumpkin or other vegetables, or legumes such as chickpeas. However, these dishes are only incidentally meat-free: Tanzanians generally find the idea of vegetarianism to be incomprehensible or silly. There is a small community of Indians along the coast, and as a consequence Indian restaurants (usually offering vegetarian dishes) are located in Dar es Salaam, Zanzibar, and elsewhere in the east. European food is served in hotels and game lodges, and in some restaurants in Dar, although vegetarian food is rarely a priority.

Swahili (p. 151) is the national language, although most Tanzanians speak something else as a native tongue. **English** is also an official language.

Uganda

Overall, Ugandan food is edible but not particularly inspiring. Starch with meat is standard restaurant fare, but all is not lost for vegetarians. There are some interesting meatless dishes such as *mugoyo* (sweet potato and white bean loaf), plantains served with peanuts, and plain sweet potatoes and rice. Some types of soup are made with vegetables or greens, but these are not always easy to find outside Ugandan homes. Pesco-vegetarians will find plenty of fish near the lakes. There are a few Indian restaurants in the towns, and Kampala has a decent selection of Western food such as pasta.

English is the official language, and most Ugandans can speak it at least at a rudimentary level. Various indigenous languages are spoken as mother tongues around the country. Swahili (p. 151) can be very useful, especially in the eastern part of the country.

C. CENTRAL AFRICA

As elsewhere in Africa, starches with stews and sauces are the basis of the Central African diet. Cassava is the cheapest and therefore the most common starch, although rice, yam, and corn (maize) are also widely used. Stews and sauces usually contain meat or fish, although some are based solely on vegetables, greens, or peanuts. Much of Central Africa is tropical forest (although given the current rate of deforestation that is likely to change), and the denizens of the jungle—monkey, chimpanzee, crocodile, or even boa constrictor or elephant—are sometimes encountered on a plate. Because of deforestation, and likely also because people persist in eating them, these animals are becoming rare and are not served as frequently as they once were.

Cameroon

Cameroon has some of the best food in Central Africa. Typical starches include rice, millet "couscous" (nothing like the North African variety), and *pâtes* made from cassava, corn (maize), plantain, banana, and yam. The accompanying sauces are often delicious and complex, but frequently contain meat. Some tomato-based sauces are meatless. Okra, cassava leaf salads, or other vegetables and greens are often served as side dishes. Forest animals such as monkeys and more obscure creatures are often eagerly served up to foreigners in a mistaken belief that all tourists want to devour the local fauna. In Yaoundé and Douala there are some European-style cafes and other eateries that offer basic Western food.

Cameroon is a federation of former English and French colonies, so **English** and **French** (p. 66) are the official languages. However, English is not spoken much except in the western part of the country, while French is spoken in the rest of Cameroon. More than 20 major indigenous languages are spoken, including Pulaar (p. 139) and Hausa (p. 140). Arabic (p. 110) is spoken by some groups in the far north.

Central African Republic

The C.A.R. is quite poor, and the available food reflects this poverty. Apart from a few European restaurants in Bangui, most eateries serve meat or sometimes fish, with assorted starches and vegetable side dishes. Typical dishes include *gozo* (manioc paste), *ngunza* (manioc leaf salad), and assorted products of cassava. Greens-based soups such as spinach stew are fairly common, but sometimes contain chicken or other meat.

French (p. 66) is the official language, but the national language is **Sangho**. Arabic (p. 110) and Swahili (p. 151) are spoken in the far east of the country.

Sangho

I would like something without _____.	Mbi ye ti te mbeni ye ti sengue na _____ pepe.	mBEE yay tee tay mBAY-nee yay tee SAYN-gay nah _____ pay-pay.
I do not eat _____.	Mbi te ye so _____ pepe.	mBEE tay yay soh _____ pay-pay.
I eat _____ and _____.	Mbi te _____ si _____.	mBEE tay _____ see _____.
meat	nyama	nyah-mah
chicken	kondo	kohn-doh
fish	soussou	soo-soo
eggs	parati kondo	pah-rah-tee kohn-doh
Thank you	Singuila	seen-GEE-lah

Chad

Chad is a poor, dry country with few natural resources or crops. The diet consists mainly of rice or millet with vegetables and meat; lamb is the most common meat in the north, while fish predominates in the region around Lake Chad. Peanuts are often added to vegetable dishes, especially those made with zucchini (courgette) and other squashes. Okra is the standard vegetable accompaniment. Salads made from sweet potato leaves or other greens are also common, although not particularly sanitary. There are a few Western-style restaurants in N'Djamena, which cannot be counted on to offer vegetarian entrees.

French (p. 66) and **Arabic** (p. 110) are the official languages. Arabic is mainly used in the northern part of the country, while dozens of tribal languages, including Sangho (p. 157), are spoken in the south.

Congo

Congolese cuisine is not very conducive to vegetarianism. Meat or fish is the centerpiece of most dishes, and it is difficult to find anything else. One could subsist on plain cassava or yam, although such a diet is neither healthy nor pleasant. Cassava leaves or other greens are sometimes available as side dishes. Bananas and papaya are fairly easy to get. There are some European restaurants and cafes in Brazzaville, but these generally concentrate on meat or fish dishes; a few restaurants serve pasta or other meatless entrees. Western-style restaurants may not serve vegetarian dishes as a matter of course, but are often willing to make meatless dishes if specifically requested to do so.

French (p. 66) is the official language. There are many indigenous African languages; the most common are **Kikongo** in southern Congo and Lingala (p. 159) in the north.

Kikongo

I would like something without _____.	Mou zola kima ke'na _____ vé.	moo ZOH-lah KEE-mah kay-nah _____ vay.
I do not eat _____.	_____ mouké koudia vé.	_____ moo-kay KOO-dyah vay.
meat	ngombé	ngohm-bay
chicken	sousou	soo-soo
fish	mbisy	mbee-see
eggs	mêky	MAY-kee
Thank you	Matondo mingi	mah-TOHN-doh meen-gee

Congo, Democratic Republic (Zaïre)

The Democratic Republic of Congo, formerly Zaïre, is a country that has been in the process of falling apart for the last quarter-century, so one should not expect a wide variety of tasty and creative vegetarian dishes. The typical meal is rice with sauce (often peanut sauce) and some kind of meat. Goat is the most common meat, but beef, chicken, and mystery animals from the jungle are also likely to turn up. Fish is eaten along the substantial length of the country's rivers. Cassava and yams are sometimes cooked, mashed, and served like mashed potatoes. Most soups contain meat, but some are made with vegetables and greens. Nutritious but possibly unsanitary greens such as cassava leaves are fairly common. There are Indian and Lebanese restaurants in the cities, but far fewer than there once were. Kinshasa still has a few Western-style restaurants, but these should not be counted on as a source for meatless dishes.

French (p. 66) is the official language, but hundreds of indigenous languages and dialects are spoken. The most useful may be **Lingala**, which was formerly the official language of the armed forces. Kikongo (p. 158) is spoken in western parts of the country; Kirundi (p. 147) and Swahili (p. 151) can be useful in the far east.

Lingala

I do not eat _____.	Ma koliya te _____.	mah koh-LEE-yah tay _____.
I eat _____ and _____.	Ma liaki _____ ma _____.	mah lee-ah-kee _____ mah _____.
meat	gombe	GOHM-bay
or	niama	nee-ah-mah
chicken	soso	soh-soh
fish	mbiusi	mBEE-see
eggs	maki	mah-kee
Thank you	Malam	mah-lahm

Equatorial Guinea
Equatorial Guinea is not particularly cosmopolitan in its cuisine. Rice, sweet potatoes and other tubers, and bananas form the basis of the diet; these staples are supplemented by fish on Bioko (the island portion of the country) and along the coastline and rivers of the mainland. Plenty of meat is eaten in inland areas, and animals such as antelope and monkey are likely to appear on the plate at some restaurants if one is incautious. Greens and vegetables are sometimes served as side dishes or toppings, and tropical fruit is easily available.

Equatorial Guinea is unique among African countries in that **Spanish** (p. 75) is the official language. A pidgin English dialect is widely spoken. **Fang** is the predominant indigenous language on the mainland. The government has recently encouraged the use of French for better communication with Equatorial Guinea's Francophone neighbors.

Fang

I do not eat _____.	Ma jii _____.	mah jee _____.
meat	chit	chihd
chicken	kub	koob
fish	cüas	kwahss
eggs	akii kub	ah-KEE koob
Thank you	Akiba	ah-KEE-bah

Gabon
Gabon is economically better off than many of its neighbors, and as a result meat is more frequently eaten here. Most Gabonese restaurants serve meat, including some meat from forest animals (although chicken and beef are more common). In food stalls and cheaper restaurants, starches such as yams and rice are served with spicy okra or other vegetables and greens; unfortunately, meat is typically added. In Libreville there are quite a few French cafes

and restaurants which sometimes serve meatless dishes. Certain Western dishes such as omelettes or french fries are common throughout the country.

French (p. 66) is the official language, and is widely used for inter-ethnic communication. Several different African languages are used in different regions of the country; Fang (p. 160) is the most common language in the northern part of the country.

São Tomé and Príncipe

This small, lush nation of two islands offers rather few culinary enticements to strict vegetarians. Fish, usually eaten with rice or occasionally tubers, is the mainstay of the diet. Some vegetables and greens are served, and tropical fruit is available, but otherwise there is little variety in the cuisine. Vegetarian soups or stews can occasionally be found.

Portuguese (p. 73) is the official language. While Portuguese is widely spoken as a second language, most people speak a Creole language called Forro.

Forro

I do not eat _____.	A mi na come _____.	ah mee nah koo-MAY _____.
meat	cane	KAH-nee
chicken	ganha	gan-YAH
fish	peixe	pee-shee
eggs	ovo	AW-voo
Thank you (male speaker)	Obrigado	oh-bree-GAH-doh
Thank you (female speaker)	Obrigada	oh-bree-GAH-dah

D. SOUTHERN AFRICA

In general, southern Africa offers a greater variety of food than other regions of the continent in part because it is generally better-off economically than other parts of Africa. Of course, there are significant exceptions to this generalization, and the food available is not always vegetarian. (ground maize) is the main starch in this region, although rice or cassava are also used in some countries. In many southern African cities, African food is difficult to find, and Western-style food is prevalent. There are Indian restaurants in most cities in the region; these reliably serve vegetarian dishes. Cheese is more common in southern Africa than in other parts of the continent.

Away from Portuguese-speaking Angola and Mozambique, and the island nations of the Indian Ocean, English is commonly spoken in southern Africa.

Angola

Land mines are scattered all over the country as an unwelcome legacy of Angola's long civil war. As a result, there is relatively little agricultural activity in the country, so food availability and variety are limited. Fish, especially cod, is the most popular meal near the coast; freshwater fish is consumed along the rivers, and beef and goat are consumed inland. Corn (maize), rice, and cassava are basic starches; potatoes are also common in Angola, unlike in most other African nations. Bananas and coconut are relatively easy to find. European restaurants in Luanda are mostly closed, although some have reopened in the last few years. Restaurants in general tend to be very expensive.

Portuguese (p. 73) is the official language. A wide array of indigenous languages are in everyday use. Some Kikongo (p. 158) is spoken in the far north and in the Cabinda enclave.

Botswana

Botswana is no vegetarian's paradise. Landlocked and largely arid, meat is the focus of most meals, at least at restaurants and takeaways; game such as zebra and antelope is commonly purveyed to tourists. Maize porridge with beans is a standard Botswanan meal; this combination is typically served with meat or a cooked vegetable dish such as *morogo* (cooked spinach or other greens).

Such food is not universally available at restaurants, however (especially at restaurants catering to travelers); steak and chicken with french fries is more usual fare. There are Indian restaurants in the towns, and these are the surest bets for vegetarian meals (although not even all Indian restaurants serve meatless dishes). Game lodges will often serve meat-free dishes, especially if an advance request has been made.

English is the official language. The primary language of everyday communication is **Setswana**, which is the native tongue of the vast majority of the population.

Setswana

I would like something without _____.	Ke batla sengwe kana _____.	kay baht-LAH sayn-gway gah-nah _____.
I do not eat _____.	Ga ke je _____.	khah kay jee _____.
I eat _____ and _____.	Ke ja _____ le _____.	kay jah _____ lee _____.
meat	nama	nah-mah
chicken	koko	koo-koo
fish	tlhapi	taw-pee
eggs	mae	mah-ay
Thank you	Ke itumetse	kee too-MEHT-see

Comoros

Traditional Comorian cuisine is heavy on rice with fish or meat, and rather light on vegetarian dishes. Coconut is used in many Comorian dishes, and a few recipes call only for coconut and vegetables. (These are difficult to find at restaurants.) Some tropical fruit is available. Comoros is heavily touristed, and as a result there are many restaurants and hotels serving European-style food; some of these have vegetarian entrees such as pasta, but meatless dishes are generally not a high priority. There are a few Chinese and Indian restaurants lurking about.

French (p. 66) and **Arabic** (p. 110) are the official languages, although the use of French is generally disfavored. Most people speak Comorian, a blend of Swahili and Arabic, as a first language. Often, Comorians can understand basic Swahili (p. 151).

On **Mayotte**, a French overseas territory, there are many French-style cafes, bakeries, and restaurants, in addition to ordinary rice and seafood. French is spoken almost universally.

Lesotho

The standard meal in Lesotho, as in much of southern Africa, consists of *miellies* (cornmeal/ground maize), often mixed with greens, and served with a stew made from meat, beans, peas, or vegetables such as eggplant (aubergine) or potato. French fries are a common snack, and in Maseru and other towns (Lesotho has no large cities), Western-style fast food is the standard fare at most eateries. A few tourist-oriented lodges and hotels offer a more refined selection of food, including occasional vegetarian dishes.

SeSotho and **English** are the official languages.

SeSotho

As with many other southern African languages, SeSotho employs a number of "click" sounds. Because they are difficult for the average English speaker to manage, the pronunciations below omit clicks. Although you will not be speaking proper SeSotho, you should still be understood.

I would like something without ____.	Ke batla ntho ntle ____.	kay baht-lah uhn-TOH uhn-tlay ____.
I do not eat ____.	Ha ke je ____.	hah kay jee ____.
I eat ____ and ____.	Ke je ____ le ____.	kay jee ____ lih ____.
meat	nama	nah-mah

chicken	kgoho	khoh-hoh
fish	tchapi	kah-pee
eggs	mae	MAH-hee
Thank you	Kea leboha	kay-ah leh-BOH-ah

Madagascar

Most citizens of Madagascar are of Malay descent, and perhaps as a result, rice is the country's staple food. However, in other respects Malagasy cuisine bears little resemblance to southeast Asian food. Cassava and corn (maize) are common starches. Spiced meat, fish, or vegetables accompany the starches; pure vegetarian dishes are rare in restaurants. Soups are popular, and greens are sometimes available. Tropical fruit remains abundant, although the country is losing forest cover and topsoil at such an alarming rate that soon it will be fortunate to have any trees left at all. Some European food, especially French cuisine, is available in Antananarivo and other cities; there are also a few Chinese and Indian restaurants.

French (p. 66) and **Malagasy** are the official languages.

Malagasy

I would like something without _____.	Mil zavatra tsy misy _____ izaho.	mee-lah ZAH-vah-trah tsee mees _____ ee-ZAH-hoo.
I do not eat _____.	Tsy mihinana _____ izaho.	tsee mee-HEE-nah-nah _____ ee-ZAH-hoo.
I eat _____ and _____.	Mihinana _____ sy _____ izaho.	mee-HEE-nah-nah _____ see _____ ee-ZAH-hoo.
meat	hena	heh-nah
chicken	akoho	ah-koo

fish	trondro	trroon-drroo
eggs	atody	ah-TOO-dee
Please	Azafady	ah-zah-FAH-dee
Thank you	Misaotra	mee-SOW-trah

Malawi

Malawian food follows the general African model: Starch (here, usually corn/maize or pumpkin, or sometimes potato) is served with sauce or stew, which typically contains meat or fish. Some sauces are vegetarian; tomato sauce and peanut sauce are both common, and beans are sometimes used. Greens are frequently used in Malawian cooking, and kale, pumpkin leaves, sweet potato leaves, and groundnut (peanut) leaves are all pressed into service. Along the shores of Lake Malawi, fish is the ubiquitous main dish; it is sometimes difficult to get anything else. It is easy to obtain fruit, especially bananas. In Lilongwe and Blantyre there are many European-style restaurants, and even a few Indian and Chinese restaurants. These are often good places to go for meatless dishes.

English and **Chichewa** are the official languages. While most Malawians can speak one or both of these languages, several indigenous tongues besides Chichewa are in use around the country. A few people in the northeast can speak Swahili.

Chichewa

I would like something without _____.	Ndifuna kudya kuna _____.	ehn-dee-foo-nah kood-yah koo-nah _____.
I do not eat _____.	Sindikudya _____.	seen-dee-kood-yah _____.
I eat _____ and _____.	Ndikudya _____ na _____.	ehn-dee-kood-yah _____ nah _____.
meat	nyama	nyah-mah

chicken	nkuku	ehn-koo-koo
fish	somba	sohm-bah
eggs	mazira	mah-zee-rah
Please	Chonde	chohn-day
Thank you	Zikomo	zee-koh-moh

Mauritius

As one expects of island nations, seafood is the main component of Mauritian cuisine. However, a polyglot of cultures co-exist here, and there are several options for vegetarians. Much of the population is of Indian descent, and Indian food helped form the cuisine of Mauritius; consequently it is easy to get vegetarian food such as lentil-based dishes. For example, rice is the staple food, and although it is usually served with fish or fish sauce, it is generally accompanied by a range of vegetables or legumes. There are also many Indian restaurants serving traditional Indian fare, including many vegetarian dishes. Chinese restaurants are common. Although one hardly needs to resort to them, lots of restaurants serve European food, especially at hotels. Italian food is particularly popular. Fresh tropical fruit is available everywhere.

English is (theoretically) the official language of Mauritius. French and are also used, but the vast majority of Mauritians speak a **Creole** dialect derived from French.

Mauritian Creole

I do not eat ____.	Mo pa mange ____.	moh pah mahnzh ____.
meat	la viande	lah vee-AHND
chicken	poul	pool
fish	poisson	pwah-SAWN

eggs	disef	dih-zehf
Thank you	Merci	mayr-SEE

The nearby island of **Réunion** is a French overseas department. The range of produce is similar to that available in Mauritius, although there are more French-style restaurants and cafes and fewer Indian or Creole offerings. **French** (p. 66) is the official language.

Mozambique

Mozambican cuisine is somewhat more diverse than the food of many other poor African countries, and tends to be quite spicy. The basic food is beans with starch (usually rice) and meat or fish, but there are many variations on this theme. Unfortunately, most of these variations involve flesh of some kind. Seafood is king along Mozambique's lengthy coastline, while chicken is the main meat elsewhere. In restaurants, it may be difficult to get anything else, although there are some traditional vegetable side dishes such as *arroz de coco* (coconut rice) with tomatoes and chili. The countryside is still rife with landmines, so fresh local vegetables are often in short supply; the extensive flooding of croplands in early 2000 exacerbated this shortage. Plenty of coconuts and tropical fruits are available, however, and roasted cashews are a common street snack. In Maputo, an array of fancy European-style restaurants serve Portuguese, French, or Italian food; less upscale establishments serve pizza, french fries, croissants, and other potential vegetarian snacks.

Portuguese (p. 73) is the official language. Most Mozambicans can speak at least some Portuguese (although it may not be understood by everyone in remote areas). Hundreds of indigenous languages are spoken in Mozambique. Shona (p. 174) is spoken in parts of the northwestern provinces that border Zimbabwe. Some Swahili (p. 151) is used in the far north.

Namibia

As the wide variety of game dishes on menus attests, Namibians are not used to catering for vegetarian travelers. Pesco-vegetarians will find that fish is usually available in restaurants, even away from the coast. Otherwise, in most parts of the country, cheese and tomato sandwiches and sad-looking salads are the order of day for anyone who wants to avoid meat. Because of Namibia's aridity, few vegetables are grown locally. Most Namibians ordinarily eat (ground maize) porridge with beans and black-eyed peas, or sometimes cooked greens, but it is difficult to find such dishes outside Namibian homes. Somewhat more variety is available in Windhoek and Swakopmund; several restaurants in these cities are used to foreign travelers and offer meatless entrees.

English is now Namibia's sole official language. However, Namibia was occupied by South Africa for decades, and Afrikaans (p. 170) remains very useful. In addition, because Namibia was formerly a German colony, German is still used, especially in the coastal towns. Many indigenous African languages are spoken, particularly in northern Namibia.

South Africa

Although the country is by no means problem-free in any respect, South Africa is a much more vegetarian-friendly place than it was just a few years ago. In the resort towns and in large cities, especially in Cape Town and the nearby winelands, an increasing number of restaurants offer palatable vegetarian entrees, and a few vegetarian-oriented restaurants and cafes have opened. Vegetarian meals are particularly easy to find in Durban, the center of South Africa's Indian community. A national steak restaurant chain even offers a vegetarian plate. In rural areas and small towns, however, it may be difficult to find a main dish that does not contain meat (particularly beef or lamb). Usually, basic sustenance such as toasted cheese-and-tomato sandwiches is the only viable option; vegans will be in dire straits indeed.

There is a tremendous difference between "white" or "Western" food and traditional African food. Most restaurants cater to a largely white clientele (who are generally more able to afford eating out than the black majority), and serve familiar European-type foods. In many black South African eateries, however, the food is quite different: *pap* (cornmeal/ground-maize porridge, sometimes called *bap*) served with *samp* (a bean sauce) is the typical entree. Greens or vegetables are sometimes served on the side. Meat or chicken is included for anyone who can afford it (almost certainly including you); although poverty limits meat consumption among much of the population, most Africans do not sympathize with intentional vegetarianism.

There are many ethnic eateries in the cities, offering everything from Mexican to Chinese to Indonesian to Middle Eastern cuisine; most such restaurants offer vegetarian entrees. Vegetarian travelers who wish to cook for themselves will find soy burgers, soy mince, tofu sausages and the like at many supermarkets, although quality is often low. Fresh fruit and vegetables in South Africa are generally abundant and excellent.

Since the unlamented collapse of apartheid, the number of official languages has grown from two (English and Afrikaans) to eleven. **English** is spoken as a first or second (or third) language by a majority of the population. **Afrikaans** is the mother tongue of most white South Africans. It is also the first language of most mixed-race ("coloured") people in the western part of the country. If you must speak a European language to an African, English will often meet with a warmer reception than Afrikaans.

Xhosa is spoken by many Africans in the western part of the country and along the south coast. **Zulu**, which is similar to Xhosa, is spoken in the KwaZulu/Natal province in the southeast. SeSotho (p. 164) is spoken mainly in the central part of the country, and in some areas bordering Lesotho. Setswana (p. 163) is spoken in some areas in the north-central part of the country. All of these languages, and several more, are spoken in the townships around Johannesburg.

Afrikaans

I would like something without _____.	Ek will iets sonder _____ hê.	ehk vuhl ehts SOHN-duhr _____ hehr.
We would like something without _____.	Ons will iets sonder _____ hê.	ohns vuhl ehts SOHN-duhr _____ hehr.
I do not eat _____.	Ek eet geen _____ nie.	ehk eert khern _____ nee.
I eat _____ and _____.	Ek eet _____ en _____.	ehk eert _____ ehn _____.
meat	vleis	flayce

chicken	hoender	HEUN-duhr
fish	vis	fihs
eggs	eier	EYE-ehr
cheese	kaas	kahs
I am a vegetarian.	Ek is 'n vegetariër.	ehk ihss uhn veh-geh-TUH-rih-ehr
Please	Asseblief	uh-suh-BLEEF
Thank you	Dankie	DUHN-kee

Xhosa

Xhosa uses a range of different "click" sounds, which are difficult for English-speakers to manage. For ease of pronunciation, the clicks have been eliminated in the pronunciations given below. You will still be understood.

I would like something without ____.	Ndifuna nto engena ____.	ndee-FOO-nah nTOH ehn-geh-nah ____.
I do not eat ____.	Andiyityi ____.	ahn-dee-yee-chee ____.
I eat ____ and ____.	Nditya ____ nlay.	ndee-CHAH ____ nlay.
meat	inyama	een-yah-mah
chicken	inkukhu	ihn-koo-koo
fish	intlanzi	ehnt-klahn-zee
eggs	amaqanda	ah-mah-KAHN-dah
Thank you	Enkosi	ehn-kohz

Zulu

Like Xhosa, Zulu uses a variety of clicks. For simplification, these clicks have been omitted from the pronunciations below.

I would like something without _____.	Ngicela ngiphe _____ ngaphandle.	ngee-keh-lah OO-ngee-peh _____ ngah-PAHN-dlay.
We would like something without _____.	Sicela ngiphe _____ ngaphandle.	see-keh-lah OO-ngee-peh _____ ngah-PAHN-dlay.
I do not eat _____.	Angiyidli _____.	ahn-GEE-yeed-lee _____.
I eat _____ and _____.	Ngiyadla _____ ne _____.	NGEE-yah-dlah _____ nay _____.
meat	inyama	ihn-yah-mah
chicken	inkuku	ihn-koo-koo
fish	intlanzi	ihnt-LAHN-zee
eggs	amaqanda	ah-mah-kahn-dah
Thank you	Ngiyabonga	NEE-yah-bohn-gah
We thank you.	Siyabonga	SEE-yah-bohn-gah

Swaziland

Swaziland is a small country with relatively little culinary variety. The typical Swazi meal is maize porridge and stew. Generally, eateries focus on meat or chicken dishes; vegetables are rare, although cooked greens are often eaten at home and are sometimes available in restaurants. Manzini and Mbabane have the standard assortment of European restaurants. There are Chinese restaurants in the towns; these generally serve basic vegetable dishes, and are a better choice for meatless meals than many Swazi food outlets.

The official written language is **English**. In everyday conversation, most Swazis speak **siSwati**. SiSwati is essentially the same language as **Zulu** (p. 172).

Zambia

The staple in Zambia is *mielie* (cornmeal/ground-maize) porridge, which is eaten at virtually every meal. (Corn/maize is also used to make Zambia's excellent beer.) The porridge is often accompanied by or mixed with greens such as spinach or pumpkin leaves. Sometimes the porridge is topped with stew, which might be made from peanuts, beans, tomatoes, or other vegetables. In most restaurants, meat or fish is included in virtually all dishes, including vegetable dishes; food stalls are more likely to offer meatless options (for cost reasons, not because of vegetarian sensibilities). Cassava and sweet potatoes are also used as starches, especially in northern Zambia. In Lusaka and Livingstone, a few European and Indian restaurants offer meatless entrees.

    English is the official language. Many indigenous languages are spoken.

Zimbabwe

Zimbabwe's national dish is *sadza*, a maize porridge that is typically served with meat, beans, a peanut butter-based sauce, or greens such as spinach. Most small eateries serve *sadza*, but a variety of Western-style foods are also available throughout the country. Steak, for example, is unfortunately quite popular, and french fries, potato chips, and assorted junk food can be had even in small towns. In Harare and Bulawayo, Indian, Chinese, Middle Eastern and other cuisines are available, and many of these restaurants serve vegetarian entrees. Most Zimbabwean game lodges and many hotels that cater to foreign tourists offer at least one meatless option.

    English is the official language, and most Zimbabweans can speak it. **Ndebele** and **Shona** are the most common languages in everyday use. Ndebele, which is spoken in the south and west, is very similar to **Zulu** (p. 172); the languages are mutually intelligible.

Shona

I would like something without ____.	Ndirikuta chunu chisina ____.	ndee-ree-KOO-tah choo-noo chee-see-nah ____.
I do not eat ____.	Andigki ____.	ahn-dee-kee ____.
I eat ____	Ndinodyka ____.	ndih-noh-chyuh-kuh ____.
meat	nyama	nyah-mah
chicken	huku	hoo-koo
fish	hove	HOH-vay
eggs	mazai	muh-zah-ee
Please	Ndapota	ndah-POH-tah
Thank you	Tatenda	tah-TEHN-dah

Asia

Asia is the largest continent, and it harbors a correspondingly vast array of cultures, cuisines, and languages. This tremendous variety makes it difficult to generalize about the availability of meatless food. In some Asian countries, such as India, it is laughably easy to find vegetarian dishes; by contrast, it is nigh impossible to do so in parts of Central Asia. Most often, however, it is of middling difficulty to obtain vegetarian dishes—while they do not leap out at the traveler, they usually can be found with reasonable effort. Strict vegetarians may have problems in parts of southeast Asia, where fish sauce is a stealthy and omnipresent ingredient even in many vegetable dishes. In the rapidly developing economies of some east Asian countries, a greater variety of food is becoming available; Western-style food (including pasta and pizza) is increasingly popular.

There is no indigenous or European language that is particularly dominant on the continent, although certain languages are widely spoken in their own regions. English is useful in former British colonies, in tourist areas, and among many businesspeople in east Asia.

A. SOUTH ASIA

It is a fairly easy task to find meatless dishes in most of south Asia. Hundreds of millions of vegetarian Hindus (and a few vegetarian Buddhists) live in this region, and their influence spills over even into non-Hindu areas. Dishes based on rice and pulses such as lentils are staples throughout the region, and are usually available even in Muslim-majority areas. In some cases, much more elaborate and interesting vegetarian dishes can be found, and are definitely worth sampling (with caution—they are often very spicy). Cheese and yogurt are also fairly common in south Asia, although the cheese usually takes a soft, cottage cheese–like form. Western-style hard cheeses are relatively rare.

Because of the legacy of British colonialism, English is useful throughout most of south Asia, especially in the cities. In more remote areas, however, there may be few English speakers.

Bangladesh

Although there are relatively few pure vegetarians in Bangladesh, it is virtually no problem to obtain vegetarian meals. Bangladeshis eat comparatively little red meat, although fish is very common (as befits a country that is largely under water for parts of the year). Obviously, fish-eaters will have an easy time in Bangladesh, but stricter vegetarians should have no serious difficulties. Most restaurants have vegetarian dishes, and rice with *daal* (lentils) or mung beans is served at food stalls throughout the country. A variety of vegetables and interesting meatless snacks, such as *piaju* (an onion-lentil ball), are commonly available.

Bangla, or Bengali, is the national language. English is widely spoken as a second language.

Bangla

Bangla uses its own alphabet, which has been transliterated and modified in the phrases below.

I would like something without _____.	Ami _____ badey kichu khete chai.	ah-MEE _____ bah-DAY kee-choo kay-tay chye.

We would like something without _____.	Amra _____ badey kichu khete chai.	ahm-RAH _____ bah-DAY kee-choo kay-tay chye.
I do not eat _____.	Ami _____ khai na.	ah-MEE _____ kye nah.
I eat _____ and _____.	Ami _____ ebong _____ khai.	ah-MEE _____ ay-bohng _____ kye.
meat	mansho	mahn-shoo
chicken	murgi	MOOR-gee
fish	mas	muhss
eggs	dim	deem
cheese	ponir	poh-NEER
Thank you	Dhonnobad	DOH-noh-bahd

Bhutan

Assuming you can get into Bhutan (only a few thousand visitors per year are allowed in), you can bet that you will eat rice at almost every meal. The prevalence of rice is illustrated by the fact that the Bhutanese have no word for "food"; instead, the Dzongkha word for rice, "toh," is used to mean food in general. Although the Bhutanese are quite fond of meat, there are a variety of dishes that are *jhaju* (prepared without meat). Many spicy vegetable dishes are meatless, and soft cheese is often used as a sauce on meat or vegetables. *Hemadatsi*, a chili and cheese paste served with rice, is a popular fast food item (the Bhutanese equivalent of pizza or hamburger in the West). Potatoes, noodles, pancakes, and dumplings are all fairly common, although sometimes these are served with meat. In the south, lentils are the typical accompaniment to rice.

Dzongkha is the official language. Dialects of Nepali (p. 185) and Tibetan (p. 201) are also spoken.

Dzongkha

The phrases below have been transliterated from Dzongkha script. See the Note on Tonal Languages *(p. 19) in the Introduction for a description of the symbols used below. (Note however that tone is not as crucial in Dzongkha as it is in some other Asian languages such as Thai.)*

I would like something without _____.	Gna toh _____ meba za we.	**ng**nah toh _____ may-bah sah wee.
I do not eat _____.	Gna _____ me za.	**ng**nah _____ may sah.
I eat _____ and _____.	Gna _____ da _____ za we.	**ng**nah _____ dah _____ sah wee.
meat	sha	↘shah
chicken	jha sha	jah ↘shah
fish	gña sha	nyah ↘shah
eggs	gongido	goh**ng**-ee-doh
cheese	da tshe	dah ↗tsee
Thank you	Kadinche	kah-deen-chay

India

India wins the award for most vegetarian-friendly country in the world. It has over 800 million Hindus, virtually none of whom eat beef, and many of whom are strict vegetarians. India has the additional distinction of hosting the world's only beef-free McDonald's (spiced vegetable patties and lamb burgers make up the bulk of the menu). Certain standard meatless dishes are available almost everywhere in India; these include *daal* (lentils), rice, and roti bread. In some areas, nothing else (meatless or otherwise) may be readily available.

Indian cuisine at its best is inventive and complex, and dishes and ingredients can vary significantly from region to region. Southern India has the greatest concentration of strict vegetarians, and thus the greatest variety of vegetarian food. Southern Indian food tends to be extremely spicy, and is widely available as street food throughout India. It commonly takes the form of curries, pancakes or breads stuffed with spicy vegetables, and various creative incarnations of pulses served with rice. In northern India, somewhat more meat (usually lamb) is consumed, but there is still plenty of vegetarian food available, such as curried vegetables and dishes containing vegetables, cream or yogurt, and nuts. Cheese is a common ingredient in northern food; Indian cheese generally does not resemble typical Western cheese, but is more like firm, small-curd cottage cheese. The far north (Jammu and Kashmir) is home to the elaborate *wazwan* banquet, which usually features a number of meat dishes as well as plenty of vegetable dishes.

The northwest is home to most of India's Muslims, and is the region where the most meat is consumed. However, Muslims do not eat pork, and in India they tend not to consume beef. In Bengal, not much meat is consumed, although seafood is very common. A few of the Tibetans in Darjeeling are strict vegetarians, and some mock meat dishes are available there. If you desire a change of pace (although probably not from any lack of indigenous meatless options), Indian cities offer a variety of restaurants purveying the foods of Europe and North America, the Middle East, and east Asia (Chinese food is particularly common).

India has an amazing number and variety of languages, many of which have over one million native speakers. **English** is an associate official language, and is spoken by most educated Indians. However, the primary official language is **Hindi**, which is spoken as a first language by almost a third of the population, mainly in the northern half of the country. Spoken Hindi is virtually identical to Urdu, which is spoken in the west of the country. Other important languages include **Gujarati**, spoken in the Gujarat state of western India; Bangla (p. 176), spoken in the Calcutta area; **Telegu**, used in Andhra Pradesh, in the southeast; **Marathi**, spoken in Maharashtra state in the west; **Tamil**, spoken in the far southern state of Tamil Nadu; Kashmiri (p. 187), spoken in Kashmir in the far north; Sindhi (p. 187, spoken in parts of western India; **Kannada**, used in Karnataka state in the southwest; and **Malayalam**, spoken in Kerala in the far southwest. Nepali (p. 185) is used in parts of northern India. Tibetan (p. 201) is spoken by the Tibetan exile community centered in Darjeeling.

Hindi

All of the indigenous languages of India use their own writing systems. The phrases and words listed below have been transliterated into the Roman alphabet.

I do not eat _____. (female speaker)	Meñ _____ nahiñ khati.	mahn _____ nuh-heen kaht-TEE.
I do not eat ____. (male speaker)	Meñ _____ nahiñ khata.	mahn _____ nuh-heen kaht-TAH.
I eat _____. (female speaker)	Meñ _____ khati huñ.	mahn _____ kaht-TEE hoon.
I eat ____. (male speaker)	Meñ _____ khata huñ.	mahn _____ kaht-TAH hoon.
meat	gosht	gohshd
chicken	murghi	moorg-gee
fish	machhli	much-hlee
eggs	anda	uhn-dah
cheese	panir	puh-neer
I am a vegetarian.	Meñ shakahari huñ.	mahn shuh-kuh-huh-REE hoon
or	Meñ vegetarian huñ.	mahn vahg-gee-tay-ree-yuhn hoon
Thank you	Shukria	shoo-kree-yah

Gujarati

I do not eat _____. (male speaker)	Huñ _____ khato nathi.	hoon _____ KAH-toh nah-TEE.
I do not eat ____. (female speaker)	Huñ _____ khati nathi.	hoon _____ KAH-tee nah-TEE.
I eat _____ and _____.	Huñ _____ ane _____ khaoun chhu.	hoon _____ ah-nay ____ kown choo.
meat	maas	mahns
chicken	kookda	koh-koh-dah
fish	machhli	mahch-hlee
eggs	inda	ihn-dah
I am a vegetarian.	Huñ sakahari chhu.	hoon shah-KUH-huhrr-ee choo
Please	Maherbani	mayr-bah-nee
Thank you	Abhaar	AHB-hahr

Telegu

I do not eat _____.	Nenu _____ thinanu.	nay-NOO _____ tee-nah-noo.
I eat _____.	Nenu _____ thintaanu.	nay-NOO _____ teen-TAH-noo.
meat	maamsamu	mahm-sah-moo
chicken	kodi	koh-dee

fish	chepalu	chay-pah-loo
eggs	gudlu	good-loo
I am a vegetarian.	Nenu saakhahaari.	nay-NOO sah-kah-hah-REE
Thank you	Meeku naa krithagnathalu	mee-koo nah kree-tuhg-nah-tah-LOO

Marathi

I do not eat _____.	Mi _____ khaat naahi.	mee _____ kaht nah-HEE.
I eat _____ and _____. (female speaker)	Mi _____ aani _____ khaate.	mee _____ ah-nee _____ kah-TAY
I eat _____ and _____. (male speaker)	Mi _____ aani _____ khato.	mee _____ ah-nee _____ kah-TOH.
meat	maañs	mahns
chicken	kombadi	KOOM-bah-dee
fish	maasa	mah-sah
eggs	andi	uhn-DEE
I am a vegetarian.	Mi shaakaahaari aahe.	mee shah-kah-hah-REE ah-HAY
Please	Krupaya	KROO-pye-yah
Thank you	Dhanyawaad	DAHN-yuh-wahd

Tamil

I do not eat _____.	Naan _____ sapida matten.	nahn _____ sah-PEH-dah mah-TAYN.
I eat _____.	Naan _____ sapiduven.	nahn _____ saw-peuh-doo-VAYN.
meat	mamisam	mahm-sahm
chicken	kozhi	koh-lee
fish	meen	meen
eggs	muttai	moo-tye
I am a vegetarian.	Naan sutha saivam.	nahn soo-tah sye-hvahm
Thank you	Nanri	NAHN-drree

Kannada

I do not eat _____.	Nanu _____ thinnuvudhilla.	nah-NOO _____ teen-noo-voo-dehl-LAH.
I eat _____.	Nanu _____ thinnuthene.	nah-NOO _____ teen-noo-tay-nay.
meat	maamsa	mahm-suh
chicken	koli	koh-lee
fish	meenu	mee-noo
eggs	motte	moht-tay
I am a vegetarian.	Nanu sasyahari.	nah-NOO sahs-yah-hah-ree
Thank you	Dhanyavadagalu	dahn-yah-vah-dah-gah-loo

Malayalam

I do not eat ____.	Njan ____ thinnathilla.	n-jahn ____ teen-nah-teel-LAH.
I eat ____.	Njan ____ thinnarundu.	n-jahn ____ teen-nah-roon-doo.
meat	irachi	ee-rah-chee
chicken	kozhi	koh-lee
fish	meenu	mee-noo
eggs	mutta	moo-tuh
I am a vegetarian.	Njan oru sasyabhukkanu.	n-jahn oh-roo sahs-yahb-boo-kah-noo
Thank you	Nanni	nah-nee

Maldives

Although it is the paradigm of a beautiful tropical archipelago, the Maldives has poor soil, and very few fruits or vegetables are produced locally. (Coconuts and breadfruit are the main exceptions.) The staple meal is rice and curry; sometimes the curry is meatless, although fish is the most common ingredient. Apart from this typical fare, there are relatively few options. A few Chinese restaurants can be found, as well as Indian restaurants that usually serve South Indian vegetarian food. Hotel restaurants serve Western food; Italian food is a particular favorite.

The national language is **Divehi**. Government officials can usually speak English.

Divehi

Divehi uses its own script, derived from Arabic and Sinhalese writing. The phrases below have been transliterated into the Roman alphabet.

I do not eat ____.	Aharen nukan ____.	ah-HAH-rehn noo-KUHNN ____.
I eat ____ and ____.	Aharen kan ____ adhi ____.	ah-HAH-rehn kuhnn ____ ahd-dee ____.
meat	egkamo mas	ehg-KAH-moh mahs
chicken	kukulu	koo-koo-LOO
fish	kandu mas	kahn-DOO mahs
eggs	bis	beese
Thank you	Sukuria	soo-koo-REE-ah

Nepal

It is generally very easy to get meatless dishes in Nepal. The most common meal in Nepal is rice with *daal* (lentils) and vegetable curry; it will probably be the most common meal for the majority of travelers, vegetarian or not. Other vegetable dishes, such as potatoes or carrots, are also commonly available. Although Nepalis are generally not as consciously vegetarian as many of their Indian neighbors, it is highly unlikely that meat will ever be imposed on you. Kathmandu offers a variety of cuisines, including Chinese, Indian, and Western. There are also a number of restaurants catering predominantly to European, Australian, and North American travelers; almost all of these establishments serve meatless dishes, and some specialize in vegetarian food.

Nepali is the official language. Other languages such as Tibetan (p. 201) and assorted Indic and Central Asian-derived tongues are also spoken.

Nepali

Nepali has its own script. The phrases below have been transliterated into the Roman alphabet.

I do not eat ____.	Ma ____ khandina.	muh ____ kahn-DEE-nuh.

I eat _____ and _____.	Ma _____ ra _____ khanchhu.	muh _____ rruh _____ kunch-HOO.
meat	maasu	MAH-soo
chicken	kukhura	koo-koo-rah
fish	maachhaa	MAHCH-hah
eggs	phul	fool
cheese	chij	cheedz
I am a vegetarian.	Ma saakaahaari huñ.	muh sah-kah-hah-ree hoon
Thank you	Dhanyabhad	DAHN-yahb-bahd.

Pakistan

Unlike their Hindu neighbors in India, most Pakistanis (the vast majority of whom are Muslim) eat substantial amounts of meat. Nonetheless, vegetarian options are available with a minimum of fuss. South Asian standards such as rice and *daal* (lentils), roti bread, and curried vegetables can be found throughout most of the country. Southern Pakistan has quite a few interesting vegetable side dishes that contain spinach, pumpkin, potato, or other green growing things; these become somewhat scarcer the further north you go. The cities feature a fairly wide variety of food, including Chinese, Middle Eastern, and Western cuisine.

English and **Urdu** are both official languages. In spoken form, Urdu is virtually the same as Hindi (p. 180); only the written forms differ. Other major languages include **Sindhi**, spoken in the southeast; **Kashmiri**, spoken in the far northeast; and Pashtu (p. 191), spoken in the north.

NOTE: All the languages listed below use distinct writing systems. The phrases and words have been transliterated into the Roman alphabet.

Sindhi

I do not eat _____.	Aauun _____ na khaaiindo aahiyaañ.	ah-oon _____ nah kyne-doh ah-hee-yah**n**.
I eat _____.	Aauun _____ khaaiindo aahiyaañ.	ah-oon _____ kyne-doh ah-hee-yah**n**.
meat	gosht'u	gohsht-oo
chicken	kukkarr'u	kook-kuhrr-oo
fish	machii'u	muh-chee-oo
eggs	baida	byde-duh
cheese	paneer'u	puh-neer-oo
Thank you	Meherbaanii	meh-hehr-bah-nee

Kashmiri

I do not eat _____. (male speaker)	Ba'h chhus ni _____ kheyvaan.	buh ch-hoos nih _____ kay-vahn.
I do not eat _____. (female speaker)	Ba'h chhes ni _____ kheyvaan.	buh ch-hehs nih _____ kay-vahn.
I eat _____.	Ba'h chhus _____ kheyvaan.	buh ch-hoos _____ kay-vahn.
meat	syun	syoon
chicken	kokkur	kohk-koor
fish	gaad	gahd

eggs	thul	tool
cheese	kra'r	kruhr
Thank you	Shukria	shoo-kree-uh

Sri Lanka

Almost without exception, the main meal in Sri Lanka is curry with rice. As befits an island nation, fish is often eaten with or in addition to these basics; meat is also sometimes used. Fortunately, the curry used is frequently a vegetable curry; there are plenty of Sri Lankan vegetarians, although only a minority of the population is Hindu, mainly in the northern part of the country. Lentils are also commonly eaten (usually in addition to the obligatory rice and curry). There are many types of stuffed breads, which can be delicious. In Colombo, and to a lesser extent in other Sri Lankan cities, Chinese and Western restaurants are available in case your palate needs a break from fiery spices.

Sinhalese is the official language. Tamil (p. 183) is spoken in the north of the island. English is widely spoken as a second language.

Sinhalese

Sinhalese uses its own writing system; the Sinhalese script has been transliterated into the Roman alphabet below.

I do not eat _____.	Mama _____ kanne nae.	mah-muh _____ kuh-NAY neh.
I eat _____ and _____.	Mama _____ saha _____ kanawa.	mah-muh _____ suh-huh _____ kuh-nuh-vuh.
meat	mas	muhss
chicken	kukulmas	koo-kool-muhss
fish	malu	mah-loo
eggs	bittara	bee-tuh-RUH

| Please | Karunakara | kah-roo-NAH-kah-ruh |
| Thank you | Bohoma sthuthi | boh-HOH-muh STOOT-tee |

B. CENTRAL ASIA

In the case of the six Stans (which contrary to appearances is not the name of a Hardy Boys mystery), vegetarians must take care not to be overly particular. This part of the world comprising Afghanistan, Kazakhstan, Kyrgyzstan, Tajikistan, Turkmenistan, and Uzbekistan, is the home of hard-fighting, hard-riding, and hard-living people who are unlikely to be sympathetic to vegetarian sensibilities about eating animals. In fact, meat, along with fermented milk, forms the core of the diet in much of the region. Since these countries are overwhelmingly Muslim, eating pork usually will not be a concern. In very remote areas with a tradition of aggressive hospitality, it might be best to give up vegetarianism temporarily (it has been reported some travelers have actually been threatened by nomads with whom they refused to share meat). Otherwise, it is possible to live (although not happily) on starches. In some areas, excellent melons, apricots, grapes, apples, and other produce are available during the summer and fall.

Thanks to past Soviet domination and occupation, Russian (p. 100) is commonly spoken as a second language throughout central Asia. Very little English is spoken.

NOTE: Most of the languages in this region use the Cyrillic alphabet, but are theoretically in the process of Romanizing their writing systems. Therefore, the words and phrases below have been presented (perhaps over-optimistically) in the Roman alphabet.

Afghanistan

Here, as elsewhere in Central Asia, lamb and other meats form the core of the diet. However, Afghanistan is probably the most vegetarian-friendly (or more accurately, least vegetarian-hostile) country in the region. Traditional Afghan cuisine includes a number of vegetable dishes containing, for example, eggplant (aubergine), pumpkin, or potatoes. Lentil and split pea dishes are fairly common, although these may be cooked in meat stock. Almost everything is served with unleavened bread or rice; sometimes plain rice gets gussied up into fancier forms. Other options may include vegetable soup (but beware of meat stock), *boulani* (turnovers, usually filled with vegetables), or Afghan noodles. Kabul formerly offered a cosmopolitan array of cuisines; however, two decades of war have understandably changed things dramatically.

Dari, a dialect of Persian, is spoken by over half the population. **Pashtu** is spoken by another third. Other Persian dialects and Central Asian languages, including Uzbek (p. 197) and Turkmen (p. 195), are spoken by the remainder of the population. Both languages use their own writing systems, which have been transliterated into the Roman alphabet below.

Dari

I do not eat _____.	Man nemeekhoram ____.	mahn neh-mee**kh**-oh-rahm ____.
I eat _____ and _____.	Man ____ wo ____ meekhoram.	mahn ____ woh ____ mee**kh**-oh-rahm.
meat	goosht	goosht
chicken	morgh	mohrk
fish	mahi	mah-HEE
eggs	tokhme-morgh	toh**kh**-meh mohrk
cheese	panir	pah-NEER
Please	Lotfan	loht-FAHN
Thank you	Mamnun	mahm-NOON

Pashtu

I do not eat _____.	Za'h _____ na khoram.	zah _____ nah **kh**ohd-rahm.
meat	wokha	woh**kh**-hah
chicken	chargha	chahr-gah
fish	mahi	mah-hee
eggs	eggae	eh-gay
I am a vegetarian.	Za'h yu zabzikore yem.	zah yoo zuhb-zee-kohr yehm

Kazakhstan

It is virtually anathema not to eat meat in Kazakhstan. Indeed, the conspicuous consumption of meat is something of a ritual, and some Kazakhs may take offense—or at least think you foolish and rude—if you do not partake. Since Kazakhstan has a large Russian Orthodox minority, in theory meatless dishes should be available during traditional fasting periods; in practice, such dishes usually are found only in private homes. Cheese, yogurt, and other products made from sheep's milk are common. There are plenty of starches, mainly rice and potatoes, to provide carbohydrates. In the summer, a wide variety of fruits, vegetables, and nuts can be bought in markets, although restaurants do not always take advantage of this bounty. Apples are available in the autumn. Finally, pesco-vegetarians will find plenty of dried fish on offer. (This fish is intentionally dried for consumption; any incidental dead, dry fish left behind by the rapid shrinking of the Aral Sea probably should be avoided.)

Kazakh is the official language, but is spoken as a mother tongue by less than half the population. The main language of commerce and inter-ethnic communication is Russian (p. 100); which is spoken as a first or second language by over two-thirds of the population. Other Central Asian languages and Slavic languages are also spoken.

Kazakh

I would like something without ____.	____ tamaq bolsa jeymin.	____ tah-mahk bohl-sah zhay-meen.
meat	etsiz	eht-SEEZ
chicken	tawïqsïz	tah-weuk-SEUZ
fish	balïqsïz	bah-leuk-SEUZ
eggs	jumïrtqasïz	zhuh-meurt-kah-SEUZ
cheese	sïrsïz	seur-SEUZ
or	qurïtsïz	koo-reut-SEUZ
I do not eat ____.	Men ____ jemeymin.	mehn ____ zhay-may-meen.
I eat ____ and ____.	Men ____ jäne ____ jeymin.	mehn ____ zhuh-neh ____ zhay-meen.
meat	et	eht
chicken	tawïq	tah-WEUK
fish	balïq	bah-LEUK
eggs	jumïrtqa	zhoo-meurt-KUH
cheese	sïr	seur
or	qurït	koo-REUT
Thank you	Raxmet	rah**kh**-meht

Kyrgyzstan

Kyrgyzstan is a paradise for confirmed carnivores; it is much like hell for vegetarians. The diet is centered on meat, especially lamb and mutton. The meat is usually accompanied by fermented sheep, goat, or camel milk, and yogurt is sometimes available. The milk is also made into cheese, and imported Russian cheese is also available. Obviously, vegans are in for an especially nasty time. Vegetables are few and far between at restaurants, although they can be found at markets in the summer. Rice and other starches are fairly common. Vegetarians who want any variety or nutritional value in their diet would be wise to bring cooking equipment and vitamin supplements.

Kirghiz is the official language, and is the mother tongue of slightly more than half the population. Russian (p. 100) is widely used. A small minority speaks Uzbek (p. 197).

Kirghiz

I would like something without ____.	____ tamak bolso jeymin.	____ tah-mahk bohl-soh dzhay-meen
meat	etsiz	eht-SEEZ
chicken	tooksuz	toh-ohk-SOOZ
fish	balïksiz	bah-leuk-SEEZ
eggs	jumurtkasïz	dzhoo-moort-kah-SEUZ
cheese	sïrsiz	seur-SEEZ
or	kurutsuz	koo-root-SOOZ
I do not eat ____.	____ jebeym.	____ dzheh-baym.
I eat ____ and ____.	____ jana ____ jeym.	____ dzhah-nah ____ dzhaym
meat	et	eht

chicken	took	toh-ohk
fish	balïk	bah-LEUK
eggs	jumurtka	dzhoo-moort-KAH
cheese	sïr	seur
or	kurut	koo-ROOT
Thank you	Ïrakmat	EU-rahk-maht

Tajikistan

As elsewhere in Central Asia, meat forms a large part of the Tajik diet. However, Tajik cooking has been modified by Persian, Indian, and Chinese influences, so the range of choices is somewhat wider than in other former Soviet republics. Vegetable dishes are actually relatively common, although meat is sometimes added. Curries, *nan* (unleavened bread), rice and lentils, and other Indian-type food is sometimes available. Rice is the most widely used starch, and it is sometimes made into pilafs or other more complex dishes; these often contain meat or are made with meat stock, however. Outdoor markets are a good source for fresh vegetables and fruit in summer.

Tajik, a Persian dialect, is the official language. Russian (p. 100) is still widely spoken as a second language. About a quarter of the population speaks Uzbek (p. 197).

Tajik

I do not eat _____.	_____ nämixoräm.	_____ nuh-mee**kh**-oh-ruhm.
I eat _____ and _____.	_____ wo ___ mixoräm.	_____ woh ___ mee**kh**-oh-ruhm.
meat	gušt	goosht
chicken	morgh	mohrk
fish	mahi	mah-hee

eggs	toxmä	toh**kh**-mah
cheese	panir	pah-neer
Please	Lotfen	loht-FEHN
Thank you	Motşäkäräm	moht-shuh-kuh-ruhm

Turkmenistan

Vegetarians in Turkmenistan deserve hardship pay, because the Turkmen diet consists almost exclusively of meat and milk products. Commonly consumed meats include camel, horse, lamb, and mountain goat. This fleshy diet is supplemented by the fermented milk of sheep, goats, and camels, and sometimes bread or rice. It is certainly possible to subsist on these supplements, although it may not be to everyone's liking. (Vegans, of course, will be especially deprived.) A few soups or more elaborate rice dishes make their appearance from time to time, although these are likely to contain meat or at least meat stock. Fish are eaten along the Caspian Sea, so pesco-vegetarians can find some relief there.

Turkmen is the national language. Almost everyone can speak Russian (p. 100) as a first or second language. There is also a minority population of Uzbek (p. 197) speakers.

Turkmen

I would like something without _____.	_____ nahar bolsa īyerin.	_____ nah-hahr bohl-sah eye-yeh-REEN.
meat	etsiz	eht-SEEZ
chicken	tovuksïz	toh-vook-SEUZ
fish	balïksïz	bah-leuk-SEUZ
eggs	yumurtğasïz	yoo-moort-gah-SEUZ

cheese		sïrsïz	seur-SEUZ
	or	päynirsiz	pay-neer-SEEZ
I do not eat ____.		____ īymerin.	____ eye-meh-reen.
I eat ____ and ____.		____ ve ____ īyerin.	____ veh ____ eye-yeh-reen.
meat		et	eht
chicken		tovuk	toh-VOOK
fish		balïk	bah-LEUK
eggs		yumurtğa	yoo-moort-gah
cheese		sïr	seer
	or	päynir	pay-NEER
Thank you		Täşäkkür	tuh-shuhk-KOOR

Uzbekistan

While Uzbeks are as fond of meat as any self-respecting Central Asian people, vegetarians will find Uzbekistan to be relatively manageable, especially in the summer. For a start, over 1000 varieties of melons are grown here. A fitting variety of other fruits and vegetables are also cultivated, and in Uzbekistan these are often incorporated into common dishes. Pumpkin, eggplant (aubergine), and spinach are all typical ingredients, and plain steamed vegetables are sometimes available as a side dish. (Variety is substantially lessened during the winter months.) Legumes such as lentils and mung beans are often served with rice. Rice pilaf is common, but is usually cooked in meat stock. A common snack is *samsa*—small pies, usually with meat fillings, but occasionally filled with vegetables. Unleavened nan bread is a standard accompaniment to most meals.

Uzbek is the principal language. Russian (p. 100) is spoken as a first language by a small ethnic Russian minority, and as a second language by much of the population.

Uzbek

I would like something without ___.	___ aş bolsa yermän.	___ ahsh bohl-sah yehr-MUHN.
meat	etsiz	eht-SEEZ
or	gössiz	gohsh-SEEZ
chicken	tavuksiz	tah-vook-SEEZ
fish	baliksiz	bah-leek-SEEZ
eggs	tuxumsiz	too**kh**-oom-SEEZ
cheese	sïrsiz	seer-SEEZ
or	kurutsiz	koo-root-SEEZ
I do not eat ___.	___ yemäsmän	___ yeh-muhs-muhn.
I eat ___ and ___.	___ vä ___ yermän	___ vuh ___ yehr-muhn.
meat	et	eht
or	göş	gohsh
chicken	tavuk	tah-VOOK
fish	balik	bah-LEEK
eggs	tuxum	too**kh**-OOM
cheese	sïr	seer
or	kurut	koo-ROOT
Thank you	Raxmat	rah**kh**-mah
or	Täşäkkürt	tuh-shuhk-koor

C. NORTHEAST ASIA

On the whole, the countries of northeast Asia do not present insurmountable hurdles to visiting vegetarians. Despite substantial Buddhist influence, vegetarianism as such is not widely practiced. However, meat traditionally has not been the centerpiece of most cuisines in this region (with the exception of Mongolia). In addition, many northeast Asians will eat occasional vegetarian meals for health or spiritual reasons, so a request for a meatless meal is not considered particularly bizarre in itself. Life is especially easy for pesco-vegetarians in most areas, because fish is often an integral part of the diet. Rice is available almost everywhere, and while it can always serve as a vegetarian last resort, it can also become tiresome quickly.

Dairy products are not normally consumed in this part of the world, and items like cheese are usually only found in Western restaurants or in some supermarkets. ("Cheese eater" is sometimes used in China as a pejorative term for a Westerner.) Eggs are very commonly eaten in northeast Asia.

China (People's Republic)

As one would expect in such a vast country, traditional Chinese cooking varies from one region to another, from the carbohydrate-heavy foods of the north to the notoriously spicy food of Sichuan in the south. Unfortunately for vegetarians, most of the regional cuisines work most of their magic with dishes that include at least some meat. It is certainly possible to get vegetarian food in China, but vegetarians will tend to miss out on the subtleties of regional variation. (This may be a good thing: Do you really care to relish the different techniques used to cook chicken feet?)

That said, many Chinese will take short vacations from meat consumption for reasons of health and balance. (The idea of permanent, intentional vegetarianism remains poorly understood, however.) To facilitate this practice, some vegetarian restaurants have sprung up, and although they are not ubiquitous, they can be found in most cities. Chinese vegetarian cooks are esteemed for the degree to which vegetarian food can be made to resemble meat, so you should not necessarily be alarmed if you are served a so-called vegetarian dish that looks like it has chunks of chicken in it. Even away from specialty vegetarian restaurants, it should not be a Herculean task to obtain meatless food. Stir-fried vegetables or bean curd (tofu) dishes are fairly easy to find. Of course, rice is served with most meals. Noodles are also very common, but they are sometimes served in broth.

A somewhat greater range of offerings is available in the larger cities. **Hong Kong** has the greatest variety of restaurants by far: Vegetarian restaurants, Indian restaurants, European restaurants, American fast-food chains, restaurants serving dishes from all the regions of China and elsewhere in east Asia are all thick on the ground. Whether such bounty will continue to be available in the next few years of Chinese rule remains to be seen. Other Chinese cities are far less cosmopolitan. Beijing has a decent selection of Asian and Western restaurants, and booming Shanghai has a burgeoning culinary scene in which many cuisines are represented. Western-style food can be found in most other eastern cities, at least in hotels, but the range of food on offer is usually limited. **Macau**, a former Portuguese colony that returned to Chinese rule in 1999, has many Portuguese and other Western restaurants (as well as restaurants serving southern Chinese–style cuisine).

In mainly Buddhist Tibet, vegetarianism is not common, but it is generally respected. Common vegetarian dishes include vegetarian dumplings, meatless noodle soup, and fake meat (for the monks). Barley dishes, grain porridges, vegetable potstickers (*sei mo-mo*), and stir-fried or steamed vegetables are also common. Dairy products are uncommon in China, although yogurt and fermented milk are eaten in western China.

Chinese is not a single language, but is divided into different dialects. **Mandarin** (also called *Putonghua*, or common language) is the official language, and most Chinese can speak it, at least as a second language. There are many additional—and mutually incomprehensible—dialects spoken around the country. The most prominent is **Cantonese**, which is spoken in Guangdong province and in Hong Kong. Assorted other non-Chinese languages are spoken by minority groups; these include Korean (p. 206), **Tibetan** in Tibet (although the Chinese government has been trying for years to eliminate its use), and **Uygur**, spoken by Central Asian Muslims in the far west and northwest of the country. Outside of Hong Kong, relatively little English is spoken except by university students and workers in the tourist industry. Many residents of Macau can speak the former official language, Portuguese (p. 73).

NOTE: All Chinese languages employ their own writing systems, which have been transliterated in the phrases below. (Uygur is often Romanized, however.) See the *Note on Tonal Languages* (p. 19) in the Introduction for a description of the symbols used below.

Mandarin

I would like something without _____.	Wo xiang chi dianr bu dai ____ de.	wǒh shěeahng ^chee deeanzh ↗boo ↘dye ____ deu.
I do not eat _____.	Wo bu chi ____.	wǒh ↘boo ^chee ____.
I eat _____ and _____.	Wo chi ____ he ____.	wǒh ^chee ___ ↗heu ___.
meat	rou	↘roh
chicken	ji	jee
fish	yu	↗eu
eggs	dan	↘dahn
I am a vegetarian.	Wo chi su.	wǒh ^chee ↘soo
Thank you	Xiexie	↘sheah-sheah

Cantonese

I do not eat _____.	Ngo hmm sic ____.	↗ngoh ↘umm sihk ____.
I eat _____ and _____.	Ngo sic ____.	↗ngoh ^sihk ____.
meat	yuk	yohk
chicken	gai	gye

fish	yui	↗jooee
eggs	dan	dahn
I am a vegetarian.	Ngo sig tsai.	↗ngoh sihk ^dzye
Thank you (for making a simple request or buying something)	Hmm goi	↘umm ^goy
Thank you (when receiving a gift or special favor)	Doh tse	^doh ^dzeh

Tibetan

In Tibetan, tones are not nearly as important as they are in Chinese or Cantonese. If you fail to use them, you will still be understood; you will merely sound peculiar. All English speakers know at least one Tibetan word: yak means yak.

I do not eat _____.	Nga _____ sa gi mei.	**ng**ah _____ suh gee may.
I eat _____.	Nga _____ sa gi yö.	**ng**ah _____ suh gee yeu.
meat	sha	shuh
chicken	cha	chuh
fish	nya	nyuh
eggs	go nga	goh **ng**ah
Thank you	Tü ji che	too jee cheh

Uygur

I do not eat _____.	_____ yemäsmän.	_____ yeh-muhs-muhn.
I eat _____ **and** _____.	_____ vä _____ yermän.	_____ vuh _____ yehr-MUHN.
meat	et	eht
chicken	toxu	toh-**KH**OO
fish	beliq	beh-LEEK
eggs	tuxum	too-**KH**OOM
cheese	kurut	koo-ROOT
_or_	irimčk	ee-reem-CHEEK
Thank you	Räxmät	rah**kh**-maht

Japan

The price of beef in Japan might drive the most ardent carnivore to vegetarianism. However, there is surprisingly little intentional vegetarianism among the Japanese. Pesco-vegetarians will find Japan to be almost heaven (and those who eat _fugu_ fish, deadly if improperly prepared, might well go the extra distance). Those who avoid flesh entirely will have a harder time, but should be able to eat reasonably well. Cooked vegetables, such as boiled spinach, are available as side dishes in most restaurants. Heartier sustenance is provided by the amazing variety of Japanese noodles. The two main varieties are _udon_ noodles, made from wheat flour, and _soba_ noodles, made from buckwheat flour; however, they are usually dipped in sauce or served in broth that is not necessarily vegetarian. Rice is of course ubiquitous, and is typically served plain, although this may not be the most satisfying meal. Another common food is _tempura_, vegetables or seafood dipped in batter and deep-fried in vegetable oil. There are many varieties of vegetable or soy soups, but chicken broth is often added. Some sushi is made of raw vegetables rather than raw fish.

World cuisines are well-represented in Japanese cities. Restaurants serving other Asian cuisines are particularly common, and these often feature meatless dishes. Italian restaurants and other Western-style restaurants are found in urban areas, although they tend to be very expensive.

Most restaurants in Japan have window displays of plastic or wax replicas of the dishes they serve. While the presentation may not be the most appetizing, and it is not always easy to distinguish vegetarian from non-vegetarian dishes, the displays make life slightly easier for befuddled or culture-shocked travelers.

Japanese is the national tongue. Many Japanese learn English in school, but they are not always proficient at speaking it.

Japanese

Japanese uses a complex set of characters; the phrases below have been converted to the Roman alphabet.

I would like something without ____.	____ no haittenai shina o kudasai.	____ noh HYE-tay-nye shee-NAH oh KOO-dah-sye.
I do not eat ____.	Watashi-wa ____ o tabemasen.	WAH-tah-shee wah ____ oh tah-bay-mah-sehn.
I eat ____ and ____.	Watashi-wa ____ to ____ tabemas.	WAH-tah-shee wah ____ toh ____ tah-bay-mahss.
meat	niku	NEE-koo
chicken	toriniku	TOH-dee-nee-koo
fish	sakana	sah-kah-nah
eggs	tamago	TAH-mah-goh
cheese	chizu	CHEE-zoo
I am a vegetarian.	Watashi-wa saishoku-shugisa desu.	WAH-tah-see wah SYE-shoh-koo shoo-GEE-sah dehss.

Please (used only if asking for a special favor; not to be used casually)	Onegaishimasu	oh-nay-gye-shee-mahss
Thank you	Arigatou gozaimasu	ah-dee-gah-toh goh-zye-ee-mahss

Mongolia

The word "variety" does not usually come to mind when trying to describe the diet of a vegetarian in Mongolia. The country is almost entirely rural, and many Mongolians still live nomadic, pastoral lives. Most Mongolians make do with mutton combined with various bland starches (especially potatoes), cabbage, and yogurt and hard cheese; a vegetarian will have to subsist on a standard Mongolian diet, minus the mutton. Because the country has no seacoast and is quite arid, fish does not figure prominently in Mongolian cuisine except near lakes. Ulan Bator is marginally more cosmopolitan than the rest of the country, and some Western, Russian, and Chinese food is available. However, even in the capital, the smell of mutton hangs heavily in the air. As Mongolia emerges further from its Soviet-imposed isolation, more culinary choices presumably will become available to the traveler.

Mongolian (Khalka Mongol), a Turkic language, is the national tongue. Russian (p. 100) is a common second language, especially among older people. A few other Turkic languages are spoken.

Mongolian

Traditional Mongolian script is beautiful and ornate, but its use has been discouraged over the last 50 years in favor of Cyrillic. However, the traditional script is once again becoming popular, and the Roman alphabet is also more commonly seen. The words and phrases below are the Romanized versions of Mongolian script.

I do not eat _____.	Bi _____ iddeggûi.	bih _____ ihd-deh-KWEE.
I eat _____ and _____.	Bi _____ iddeg.	bih _____ ihd-dehk.

meat	max	mah**kh**
chicken	taxia	tah**kh**-ee-ah
fish	zagas	zah**kh**-ahss
eggs	ōndog	ohn-duhk
cheese	byaslag	BEE-ah-slahk
Thank you	Bayarlalaa	bye-ahr-lah-LAH

North Korea

While North Korea may be a mystery wrapped inside an enigma, the food is no surprise: Rice, when it is available, is the staple of the North Korean diet. In those rare times when there is enough for all to eat, North Korean food is similar to that of its counterpart south of the DMZ. When harvests are poor (as they often have been in recent years), vegetarians are unlikely to have any problem avoiding meat: North Korean television has been known to broadcast tips on "tasty ways to prepare grass." It is best for travelers to avoid North Korea altogether at such times.

Korean (p. 206) is the national language.

South Korea

Traditionally, meat has not been the focus of Korean cuisine, but unfortunately it has become very common in the last quarter-century. Rice remains the centerpiece of the meal, so it is always possible (although boring and not particularly healthy) to eat plain rice. Rice in its various permutations is served with side dishes, which are sometimes meatless, but more frequently do contain meat. The most famous vegetable dish is probably the notorious fermented *kimchi*, which can be made from one of several kinds of vegetables, usually cabbage. (A few varieties may contain fish.) Other possible side dishes include seasoned vegetables, or tofu or vegetable stews and soups. Unfortunately, many of the soups contain meat or fish or are made with meat stock. Noodles made from wheat, buckwheat, or potato are fairly common, but may be served with meat or meat broth.

It can be difficult to find any substantial vegetarian options at many restaurants, as main courses are almost uniformly meaty, and even vegetable side dishes may contain meat or fish. (Pesco-vegetarians should survive well in most places.) Some back-alley restaurants pose further dangers by serving esoteric foods such as dog or earthworm soup. If it proves positively impossible to find a vegetarian option at a Korean restaurant (or if rice with vegetables becomes tiresome), other cuisines are well-represented in the cities. Chinese, Japanese, and all manner of Western food is commonly available.

The national language is **Korean**.

Korean

Korean uses its own alphabetical system, which has been transliterated into the Roman alphabet below.

I would like something without _____.	Nanŭn _____ an dŭrŏhgan gŏsul mŏkgo shipsŭm-nida.	nah-neun _____ ahn teu-loh-gahn keu-seul muh-koh shihp-seum-nee-dah.
We would like something without _____.	Wurinŭn _____ an dŭrŏhgan gŏsul mŏkgo shipsŭm-nida.	woo-ree-neun _____ ahn teu-loh-gahn keu-seul muh-koh shihp-seum-nee-dah.
meat	kogi-ga	koh-kee-kah
chicken	takgogi-ga	tah-koh-gee-kah
fish	saengsŏn-i	sahng-suhn-ee
eggs	kyeran-i	geh-rahn-ee
I do not eat _____.	Nanŭn _____ an mŏksŭmnida.	nah-neun _____ ahn muhk-seum-nee-dah.
I eat _____.	Nanŭn _____ mŏksŭmnida.	nah-neun _____ muhk-seum-nee-dah.

meat	kogi-rŭl	koh-kee-leul
chicken	takgogi-rŭl	tah-koh-gee-leul
fish	saengsŏn-ŭl	sahng-suhn-eul
eggs	kyeran-ŭl	geh-rahn-eul
I am a vegetarian. (This phrase implies that the speaker eats no animal products whatsoever.)	Nanŭn chaesik chuŭija imnida.	nah-neun cheh-sihk joo-oy-chah ihm-nee-dah.
Thank you	Kamsahamnida	kahm-sah-hahm-nee-dah

Taiwan

Taiwanese food does not vary dramatically from the food consumed across the Taiwan Straits in the People's Republic. While meat and fish are very common, items such as stir-fried vegetables, noodles, and bean curd are also easily available. Many Taiwanese occasionally abstain from meat, and most cities and even some smaller towns have vegetarian restaurants. Generally, mock meat made from soya is served at these establishments, although more vegetable-oriented dishes are also available. Many ordinary restaurants will also serve meatless dishes upon request. Rice, of course, is available everywhere and served with everything.

Taiwan is somewhat more Westernized than the People's Republic, and it is easy to find Western-style fast food as well as more formal establishments serving European or American dishes. Taipei and Kaohsiung are good places to seek variety. Other Asian cuisines are well-represented, especially in the cities.

Mandarin Chinese (p. 200) is the official language, and virtually everyone on the island can speak it as a first or second language. Many people speak other Chinese dialects, especially Taiwanese or Hakka, as a first language.

D. SOUTHEAST ASIA

In theory, southeast Asia should be easy pickings for vegetarians: fresh vegetables are common ingredients, tropical fruit is bountiful, and vegetable oil is usually used for cooking. In practice, however, southeast Asian cuisine poses hidden culinary perils. Chicken, pork, and beef are well-loved (as are many animals less familiar to Westerners), but are easy enough to spot and avoid. The real problem arises from the use of seafood, particularly fish sauce. In many parts of the region, fish sauce is added liberally to all sorts of dishes, and it is often difficult to determine which food contains fish sauce and which does not. (Obviously, this will not be a problem for pesco-vegetarians.)

There are a few vegetarian restaurants scattered around the region's main cities. In areas frequented by Western travelers, many restaurants offer meatless dishes. Chinese restaurants, which generally have at least one vegetarian option, can be found in most large towns. Rice is the staple food throughout southeast Asia, so it will always be possible to get your fill of this ubiquitous starch. As in other east Asian countries, cheese is not a common food.

Brunei
This tiny but rich country has rather few dining options at all, let alone fantastic offerings for vegetarians—rice and meat are the staples. If you happen to be able to eat petroleum (Brunei's main export) then you might enjoy dining here. There are a few Indian and Chinese restaurants, which are probably the only viable options for meatless entrees. There are also a few Western-style restaurants, mainly in hotels, that sometimes offer vegetarian dishes.

The official language is **Malay**, which is identical in all important respects to Bahasa Indonesia (p. 212). English is a common second language.

Cambodia
Cambodia is not a particularly vegetarian-friendly place, although there are vegetarian restaurants in Phnom Penh, Siem Reab, and a few other towns. Western-style food such as pizza is available in the cities. Apart from these urban amenities, vegetarian pickings are slim. Like every other country in southeast Asia, rice, usually served with meat, is the staple food. It is usually possible to order main dishes without meat, but the concept of vegetarianism

is difficult for most Cambodians to understand, and some people may try to slip broth or bits of meat into food to keep vegetarians from growing "too weak." With luck, despite your "weakened" state, you may stumble across indigenous vegetable dishes, such as *cha tra kouen* (fried water lily, usually served with bean paste). It is quite possible to provide for yourself (albeit leanly) here: French-style baguettes are available in most towns, all manner of luscious fruit can be found, and there are plenty of meatless snacks such as *trakoowen* (morning glories) and *sandayk dai* (peanuts). Pesco-vegetarians will have a much easier time, because fish is commonly eaten in most parts of the country.

Khmer is the official language. French is still widely used as a hangover from colonial days.

Khmer

Khmer uses its own alphabetical script, which has been roughly transliterated into the Roman alphabet below. Unlike other southeast Asian languages, Khmer is not tonal.

I would like something without _____.	Kyoum choal chit moap oait mian _____.	k-nyohm chohl cheht m-hohp OTT mee-uhn _____.
I do not eat _____.	Kyoum niam _____ mun ban te.	k-nyohm nyahm _____ meun bahn tay.
I eat _____.	Kyoum niam _____.	k-nyohm nyahm _____.
meat	sait	syet
chicken	sait mourn	syte moh-ahn
fish	trey	truh-ee
eggs	poang mourn	poh-ah**ng** moh-ahn
Thank you	Ar goun	ahr koon

East Timor

East Timor is poised to become the world's newest independent state, and an increasing range of food is becoming available in this former backwater to serve the legions of foreign aid workers, peacekeepers, and United Nations functionaries that have poured into the country to prepare it for full independence.

Although most restaurants in Dili, the capital, closed or were destroyed by rioting militias following the referendum supporting independence from Indonesia, many new restaurants have opened to serve the heavy influx of foreigners (particularly Australians and Europeans). Several of the restaurants geared to Westerners serve vegetarian dishes. A few Portuguese restaurants preserve the legacy of several centuries of Portuguese rule (although these are of minimal interest to most vegetarians).

Other restaurants offer traditional East Timorese food, which consists largely of vegetables or beans served with starches such as rice, corn (maize), or sweet potatoes; usually, the addition of a small amount of meat is deemed necessary for "flavor." However, most Timorese will be happy to leave meat out of dishes they prepare for you, even if they do not fully understand why anyone would want to avoid meat. As the country slowly rebuilds, it is likely that the variety of food available to vegetarians will gradually increase.

The various groups in this small country speak a surprising number of languages. By far the most widely spoken is **Tetum**. Most East Timorese know **Bahasa Indonesia** (p. 212), which was taught in all schools, although the use of Tetum is now preferred. Many people (especially older Timorese) may know Portuguese (p. 73), the official colonial language until the 1970s.

Tetum

I do not eat _____.	Hau la han _____.	how luh huhn _____
I eat _____.	Hau han _____.	how huhn _____
meat	naam	nuh-uhm
chicken	naam manu	nuh-uhm muh-noo

fish	ikan	ee-KUHN
eggs	manu tolum	muh-noo toh-luhm
cheese	queijo	KAY-zhoo
Thank you (male speaker)	Obrigado	aw-bree-GAH-doh
Thank you (female speaker)	Obrigada	aw-bree-GAH-dah

Indonesia

The exact range of food available in Indonesia varies from island to island and region to region. Generally, it should not be too difficult to find vegetarian dishes. While chicken and fish are standard everywhere, and obscure forest animals are eaten frequently on Borneo, they are by no means the only options available. Rice is the staple food throughout the country, but Indonesian cuisine employs lots of other grains, legumes, tubers such as cassava, and vegetables, cooked in a variety of ways (coconut milk is a particularly common ingredient). Tofu and tempeh are also widely used. One of the most well-known Indonesian dishes is *gado gado*, steamed vegetables or greens with peanut sauce; it is usually perfectly acceptable for vegetarians. The rice table is another good option: A wide selection of dishes is placed before you, many of which will probably be meatless, and you (usually) pay only for what you eat. However, in some areas of the country, fish sauce is added to many dishes and it is not immediately obvious which dishes contain this ingredient.

Most Indonesian restaurants will not mind customers asking for meatless dishes, even if nothing suitable appears on the menu. In the cities, Western food is easily available, and meatless dishes are often available there. In areas frequented by tourists, some specialty vegetarian restaurants exist, and most ordinary restaurants will serve at least a few vegetarian dishes. Bali has a particularly wide selection of vegetarian-friendly restaurants.

Dozens of languages are spoken in Indonesia. To ease inter-group communication, **Bahasa Indonesia** (often just called Bahasa) was adopted as the national tongue; it is spoken by virtually everyone in the country as a first or second language. **Javanese,** spoken (as one would expect) on Java, has the most native speakers of any Indonesian language.

Bahasa Indonesia

I would like something without _____.	Saya mahu makanan tanpa _____.	suh-yuh muh-oo muh-kuh-nuhn tuhn-puh _____.
We would like something without _____.	Kami mahu makanan tanpa _____.	kah-mee muh-oo muh-kuh-nuhn tuhn-puh _____.
I do not eat _____.	Saya tidak makan _____.	suh-yuh tee-duhk muh-kuhn _____.
I eat _____ and _____.	Saya makan _____ dan _____.	suh-yuh muh-kuhn _____ duhn _____.
meat	daging	duh-gihng
chicken	daging ayam	duh-gihng eye-yuhm
fish	ikan	ee-KUHN
eggs	telur	tuh-LOORR
cheese	keju	kay-joo
Thank you	Terima kasih	teh-REE-muh KAH-see

Javanese

Javanese has several complex levels of formalism that vary depending on the relationship between speaker and addressee. In order to avoid offense, the phrases used here are somewhat formalistic. Although you can safely use them, you may sound unnaturally stiff and distant in some contexts.

I do not eat _____.	Kula mboten . nedha ____.	koo-luh boh-tehn nehd-hoh ____.
I eat _____ and ____.	Kula nedha ____ lan ____.	koo-luh nehd-hoh ____ luhn ____.
meat	daging	duh-gihng
chicken	pipik	pee-pee
fish	iwak	ee-wuh
eggs	endog	uhn-DOHK
Thank you	Matur nuwun	MAH-toor noo-woon

Laos

Most Laotians are accustomed to eating all types of meat. As one would expect, vegetarianism is neither widely practiced nor well understood; even Buddhist monks eat meat. Pesco-vegetarians should have no problems, because fish is an extremely common food, especially in towns along waterways. Stricter vegetarians might ask for a vegetable dish such as stir-fry, but it is likely to contain oyster sauce or *nam pa* (fish sauce). Fish sauce is added to almost every recipe, although if you ask nicely people may try to accommodate you and leave the fish sauce out. Since rice is served with everything, plain rice is always an option. Sweetened sticky rice is also common.

Lao is the official language. Lao is broken up into many different dialects, some of which are closer to Thai (p. 219) than to standard Lao. There are also several minority ethnic groups with their own languages. Many older people speak French.

Lao

Lao has its own writing system, which has been transliterated into the Roman alphabet below. Lao is a highly tonal language; see the Note on Tonal Languages *(p. 19) in the Introduction for a description of the symbols used below.*

I do not eat _____.	Khoy gin _____ bo dai.	↘koy geen _____ boh ↘dye.
I eat _____ and _____.	Khoy gin _____ dai.	↘koy geen _____ ↘dye.
meat	sin	↘sheen
chicken	sin gai	↘sheen gye
fish	paa	pah
fish sauce	nam paa	↘nuhm pah
eggs	khai	kye
Thank you	Khawp jai	↘kawp jye

Malaysia

Traditional Malay cooking is not particularly oriented towards vegetarianism. Nonetheless, it is not difficult to avoid meat and eat well here. The major cities have specialty vegetarian restaurants, usually run by ethnic Chinese (who make up about a third of the population). These serve Chinese-style vegetarian food, such as mock meat and fish, or tofu and vegetables. There is a significant Indian minority in Malaysia, and consequently Indian restaurants are very common and almost always serve vegetarian dishes. Food stalls usually serve some meatless dishes such as rice and mixed vegetables. A more elaborate and fairly common offering is vegetarian banana leaf rice—rice served on a banana leaf with three different vegetable dishes. The cities and resort areas have plenty of Western-type food; pizza and pasta are particularly popular. Those who prefer to picnic will find a magnificent selection of tropical fruit. Soy milk is easily available.

Malay is the main national language. It is identical in virtually all respects to Bahasa Indonesia (p. 212). English is widely spoken in most parts of the country, especially in major cities and resort areas. A large proportion of the population is of Chinese descent; these people still speak dialects of Chinese. Many ethnic Indians speak languages such as Tamil (p. 183) and Hindi (p. 180). Tribal languages are spoken in Malaysian Borneo.

Myanmar (Burma)

Burmese cuisine is an interesting amalgam of Indian, Thai, and Chinese cooking styles. As in neighboring countries, the staple food is rice, often made into a variety of interesting dishes, such as the ubiquitous, rich and rather cloying *mon't lone yay baw* (floating rice balls). The rice is accompanied by meat or vegetable dishes. Stir-fried vegetables or greens such as watercress are quite common; unfortunately, they are often served with fish sauce. Vegetable curries are also easily available, including unusual varieties such as pumpkin curry, gourd curry, or bean curry. Again, however, fish sauce is sometimes added. Vegetable soups are common. For example, gourd soup is served in many restaurants and virtually every food stall; alas, even if soup is free of fish sauce, it normally is made with shrimp powder. There are some interesting meatless snacks, such as gourd strips with bananas in garlic and vinegar sauce, split pea or onion fritters, and steamed eggplant (aubergine).

Besides restaurants serving traditional Burmese cuisine, Indian and Chinese restaurants are very common and are good sources of meatless dishes. Indian dishes generally do not contain fish sauce. In Rangoon and Mandalay, Western food is popular, and such tasty treats as pizza and pasta are available.

Burmese is the national language. There are also several different ethnic groups which use their own languages.

Burmese

Burmese uses its own writing system; the words and phrases below have been transliterated into the Roman alphabet. Burmese is also tonal; see the Note on Tonal Languages *(p. 19) in the Introduction for a description of the symbols used below.*

I would like something without _____.	____ ma ba beh sa ba meh.	____ muh pahr beh ^sahr bah meh.

I do not eat _____. (male speaker)	Cha-naw _____ ma sa bu.	chuh NAW _____ muh sahr boo.
I do not eat ____. (female speaker)	Cha-ma _____ ma sa bu.	chuh MUH _____ muh sahr boo
I eat _____. (male speaker)	Cha-naw _____ sa ba de.	chuh NAW _____ sahr bah deh.
I eat _____. (female speaker)	Cha-ma _____ sa ba de.	chuh MUH _____ sahr bah deh.
meat	aa thaa	ah THAH
chicken	che' tha	cheht thah
fish	nga	ngah
eggs	oo	↘oh
Thank you	Che-zu tin ba de	cheh soo tihn nah deh

Philippines

The Philippines presents two faces to vegetarians. On one hand, vegetarian-ism is growing in popularity, particularly in urban areas. Most cities now have one or more specialty vegetarian restaurants, and many upscale non-vegetarian restaurants offer meatless entrees. At the same time, most Filipinos, particularly in rural areas, do not have a firm grasp of the concept of vegetarianism. For example, when ordering a "vegetarian" pizza, you might be asked what meat you would like as a topping. Rice remains the sta-ple food throughout the country, and despite the growing but still small number of vegetarians, it is usually accompanied by fish or pork. In some areas, *aso* (dog) is eaten, although the government is discouraging its con-sumption (especially in front of tourists). Vegetables (with rice) make a decent meal, but they are often served with meat or with the stealth ingre-dient *patis* (fish sauce). In towns, if no vegetarian restaurant is available, Chinese restaurants can usually be found. Also, Western-style food is always popular and may sometimes provide a meatless alternative (non-vegetarian vegetarian pizzas notwithstanding).

Tagalog is the national language. English is an official language, and many Filipinos can speak it fluently. Dozens of local languages are used in the provinces.

Tagalog

I would like something without _____.	Gusto ko po sana ng walang _____.	GOO-stoh koh poh sah-nah **ng** wah-lah**ng** _____.
We would like something without _____.	Gusto namin po sana ng walang _____.	GOO-stoh nah-meen poh sah-nah **ng** wah-lah**ng** _____.
I do not eat _____.	Hindi ako kumakain nang _____.	heen-dee ah-koh koo-mah-kah-een nah**ng** _____.
I eat _____ and _____.	Kumakain ako nang _____ at _____.	koo-mah-kah-een ah-koh nah**ng** _____ aht _____.
meat	karne	KAHR-nay
chicken	manok	mah-NOHK
fish	isda	ees-DAH
eggs	itlog	eet-LOHG
cheese	keso	KAY-soh
Please	Paki	pah-kee
Thank you	Salamat	sah-LAH-maht
Thank you (Respectful, said to elders)	Salamat po	sah-LAH-maht poh

Singapore

Singapore is a cosmopolitan and compact city-state, and many food choices are packed into its small area. The Chinese are the dominant ethnic group in Singapore and many of China's regional cuisines are represented here. Chinese-style vegetarian food is available in almost all food courts and hawker stalls, and there are several specialty vegetarian restaurants; these often make mock meat dishes (such as the seemingly oxymoronic vegetarian sweet and sour pork). There are many traditional Malay food outlets, but most specialize in poultry dishes; some vegetable side dishes are usually available, however. Plenty of Indian restaurants can be found in Singapore, and as one would expect these often serve wonderful vegetarian meals (banana leaves are sometimes used in place of plates). Other Asian and Western cuisines are easily accessible.

Singapore has four official languages: Chinese (**Mandarin** —p. 200), **Malay** (Bahasa Indonesia—p. 212), **Tamil** (p. 183), and **English**. Generally, English works well, as most Singaporeans can speak at least some English as a second language. The other languages are used by their respective ethnic groups (Chinese, Malay, and Indian).

Thailand

Despite a long Buddhist tradition, and contrary to the impression that some Thai restaurants create in the West, very little Thai food is purely vegetarian. Rice is the staple food, and while it is certainly possible to eat plain rice morning, noon, and night, such a diet would be singularly unsatisfying. Unfortunately, the available accompaniments are often not suitable for strict vegetarians. Curries are very common, but usually contain meat of some kind. (Water-buffalo curry, anyone?) Most vegetable dishes and vegetable soups contain fish sauce (*nam pla*), dried shrimp, or both, and these seafood products are not always readily discernible. However, as one might expect, pesco-vegetarians should be able to eat well anywhere in the country. Noodles and salads are sometimes meat-free and fish-free.

There are very few specialty vegetarian restaurants, but there are a growing number of "health food" restaurants that serve low-fat, high-fiber foods which are incidentally meat-free. Chinese restaurants are also fairly common, and some of these restaurants serve vegetarian entrees. In the cities, many different Asian and Western cuisines are available. Restaurants that cater to Western travelers can be found in Bangkok, Chiang Mai, Phuket, and many other popular destinations; these restaurants generally serve vegetarian dishes.

Thai is the official language. Chinese dialects, Malay (Bahasa Indonesia—p. 212), and a host of other minority languages and dialects are also spoken.

Thai

Thai employs a unique system of writing. The words and phrases below have been transliterated into the Roman alphabet. Thai is also a difficult tonal language. See the Note on Tonal Languages (p. 19) in the Introduction for a description of the symbols used below.

I would like something without _____. (male speaker)	Pohm khaw a'arai thii mii _____.	↗pohm ↗kaw ah-rye ↘tee mee _____.
I would like something without _____. (female speaker)	Diichan khaw a'rai thii mii _____.	dee ↘chuhn ↗kaw ah-rye ↘tee mee _____.
We would like something without _____.	Rau khaw a'rai thii mii _____.	row ↗kaw ah-rye ↘tee mee _____.
I do not eat _____. (male speaker)	Phom gin _____ mai dai gin.	↗pohm keen _____ ↘mye ↘dye.
I do not eat _____. (female speaker)	Diichan gin _____ mai dai gin.	dee ↗chuhn keen _____ ↘mye ↘dye.
I eat _____. (male speaker)	Phom gin _____.	↗pohm ken _____.
I eat _____. (female speaker)	Diichan gin _____.	dee ↗chuhn keen _____.
meat	nya	↘neuah

chicken	gai	kye
fish	plaa	blah
fish sauce	nam plaa	nuhm blah
eggs	khai	kye
Thank you (male speaker)	Khawp khun khrap	kawp kuhn kruhp
Thank you (female speaker)	Khawp khun kha	kawp kuhn ↘kuh

Vietnam

As elsewhere in southeast Asia, rice is the staple food and is eaten as part of virtually all meals in Vietnam. Unfortunately, meat in some form usually accompanies the rice. The Vietnamese are particularly fond of pork, chicken, and fish. While the first two creatures are easy to spot, the fish fondness can pose problems; strict vegetarians face pitfalls at every turn, because fish sauce—*nuoc nam*—is added to all sorts of otherwise innocuous vegetable dishes. More esoteric animals, including endangered species, are also eaten from time to time; the ultimate vegetarian's horror is probably the "delicacy" of monkey brains eaten directly out of the skull of a live, strapped-down monkey.

Despite the carnivorous habits of most Vietnamese, some occasionally indulge in periods of vegetarianism. Most cities have specialty vegetarian restaurants, as well as a small but rapidly increasing number of Western-style restaurants serving pizza and the like. Restaurants catering to Western travelers have opened in popular tourist centers; these usually offer at least one vegetarian entree. Outside of these areas, rice with vegetables is probably the best bet (but beware of fish sauce). Some restaurants may be willing to throw together something more elaborate for vegetarians.

Vietnamese is the official language. Various minority languages are spoken in some remote areas of the country, especially along the borders with Cambodia and Laos. There is also a small Chinese-speaking minority.

Vietnamese

Vietnamese is a tonal language; see the Note on Tonal Languages *(p. 19) in the* Introduction *for a description of the symbols used below.*

I would like something without ____.	Tôi muốn món ăn không có ____.	doy ↗moo-uhn ↗mawn ahn kowmng ↗koh ____.
I do not eat ____.	Tôi không ăn ____.	doy kohmng aan ____.
I eat ____ and ____.	Tôi ăn ____ và ____.	doy aan ____ ↘vah ____.
meat	thịt	↗teet
chicken	thịt gà	↗teet ↘gah
fish	cá	↗kah
eggs	quả trứng	kwâh ↗choouhng
cheese	phó mát	↗faw ↗maht
Thank you (addressing a man)	Cám ơn ông	↗kahm uhn ohng
Thank you (addressing a woman)	Cám ơn cô	↗kahm uhn koh

Australia and the Pacific

Although no person is an island, every country in this chapter is an island—a large island, a small island, or a group of islands. Being entirely surrounded by water, the peoples of these countries consume a good deal of fish; pesco-vegetarians should be content anywhere. Traditionally, the peoples of the Pacific island nations have eaten lots of starches—yams, taro, cassava, other root vegetables, rice, and breadfruit—supplemented by coconuts, tropical fruit, greens, and of course fish. In the last half-century, however, these traditional diets have been corrupted by the influence of North American and Australian junk food culture. In some areas, it is difficult to find traditional food, even in private homes. (Most Australians and New Zealanders, of course, have long had stereotypically "Western" diets.) On the other hand, on remote and undeveloped islands it may be difficult to find anything other than starches, fish, and fruit.

In large towns and in areas where tourists congregate, the culinary offerings may be more diverse: Chinese, Japanese, or even Indian restaurants can be found. In any case, it should not be a problem anywhere in the region to find something meatless on which to subsist (although choices may be very limited). Prospective visitors should not let dietary concerns delay their trip for too long; some observers predict that rising sea levels may engulf the most low-lying atolls sometime in the next half century.

Language
A range of Polynesian, Melanesian, Papuan, and aboriginal languages are spoken in this region. Many of these languages are spoken by only a few hundred people or even fewer, and are rapidly approaching extinction. Due to patterns of colonization, English works perfectly well as a mode of communication in most countries of the Pacific, except on the French islands.

Because there is no indigenous dairy tradition in the Pacific, few of the languages listed below have a word for cheese. Generally, the English word "cheese" (or fromage in French-speaking areas) is used.

Australia

Much of the history and folklore of Australia over the last two centuries has grown out of pastoralism, particularly cattle and sheep grazing, and Australia is home to the largest cattle stations in the world. Therefore, it should come as no surprise that Australians are ardent carnivores. Steak, lamb, or seafood (or some permutation thereof) is the centerpiece of an average Australian meal. This is especially the case in many small outback towns, where a vegetarian visitor may feel freakish and uncomfortable (although a healthy zest for beer can ameliorate local resentment). Travelers must also navigate around well-intentioned offers of such esoteric items as crocodile or kangaroo meat.

Fortunately, in the cities of Australia, there should be minimal problems in finding a vegetarian meal. Most large towns have at least one vegetarian or health food restaurant, and many ordinary restaurants are beginning to feature vegetarian entrees. There are also large Asian and European immigrant communities in the cities, particularly in Sydney, so ethnic eateries will usually be an option. Meatless meals are also relatively easy to find in the wine-producing regions of Victoria, New South Wales, Western Australia, and South Australia. Pesco-vegetarians will have an easy time virtually anywhere along Australia's coastline.

English is the principal language, and is spoken throughout Australia. Indigenous aboriginal languages are spoken in some areas of the outback and northern Queensland, while various Asian and European languages are used by immigrants to Australia.

Australia administers several overseas territories in the Indian and Pacific Oceans. The most significant of these is **Norfolk Island,** whose inhabitants grow tasty tropical fruit and speak English.

Fiji

Fijian food is somewhat more varied than the cuisine of many other Pacific nations because the population is ethnically split. Indigenous Fijians of

Melanesian-Polynesian origin and Indians who arrived as laborers in the nineteenth century each make up close to half the nation's population. Ethnic Fijians traditionally have eaten standard Pacific Island food: bread-fruit, rice, taro, cassava, fish, and assorted vegetables and greens. Fijian Indians are more amenable to vegetarianism; at Indian restaurants, rice with daal (lentils) is common, as are curries. Everyone partakes of the excellent tropical fruit in season. However, Western-style food has made considerable inroads, and American- and Australian-type fast food is very common. European, Chinese, and other Asian cuisines are also available in the towns.

English is the official language. **Fijian** is used by the ethnic Fijians, who generally can also speak English. Many Fijians of Indian descent speak Hindi (p. 180) or other Indian languages.

Fijian

I do not eat _____.	Au sega ni kana _____.	ow SAYNG-ah nee KAH-nah _____.
meat	lewe-ni-manumanu	LAY-way nee mah-noo-MAH-noo
chicken	toa	toh-wah
fish	ika	EE-kah
eggs	yaloka	yah-LOH-kah
Thank you	Vinaka vakalevu	vee-NAH-kah vah-kah-LAY-voo

The French Islands

The French still possess an array of islands in the South Pacific, which they use for benign activities such as vacationing and, until recently, testing nuclear weapons. On all of these islands, **French** is an official (if not always the preferred) language.

New Caledonia, which in turn has its own dependencies, features an international culinary atmosphere. French restaurants and bakeries dot the lush landscape. Other Western-style restaurants, such as pizzerias, are very common. Indian, Southeast Asian, and Chinese restaurants complete the picture. Many locals eat traditional Pacific Island fare: taro, manioc, and banana dishes are all common (although hard to find in restaurants).

The overseas territory of French Polynesia comprises several archipelagic groups. Tahiti is the best-known island. Excellent French restaurants and bakeries exist here, but a whole host of international offerings is also available. Chinese, Indian, Italian, and even Middle Eastern restaurants can be found. Pesco-vegetarians will find amazing seafood. On Tahiti itself, indigenous food is surprisingly hard to find (although excellent tropical fruit is always available). However, on the outer islands, standard Pacific Island food such as fish and taro are typically consumed. Most islanders speak Tahitian as a first language, but they are perfectly competent in French.

The far-flung islands of Wallis and Futuna are little visited, and the local cuisine consists of Pacific Island standards such as coconuts, yams, taro root, and bananas.

Kiribati

This nation of low-lying island groups has an intimate relationship with the sea, and fish figures prominently in Kiribatian diets. Vegetarians who would like their relationship with the sea not to involve eating its denizens may choose from the standard array of Pacific island produce: Taro, breadfruit, sweet potatoes, and assorted vegetables are grown on most inhabited islands where the soil is good enough. Rice is a common staple. Many basic foodstuffs are imported. On some islands, there are a few hotels and small restaurants that serve American-style food.

English is the official language. Most people use one of several indigenous Pacific languages at home.

Marshall Islands

Although astoundingly beautiful, the Marshalls are low-lying islands with poor soil. As a result, there are few vegetables and relatively little fruit. Apart from breadfruit and rice—and of course fish—the diet is highly

Westernized, with a disappointing amount of American fast food. A few restaurants offer more thoughtful versions of European-style food (and meatless dishes are usually available there). Otherwise, the Chinese and Japanese restaurants in the large towns are generally the best (although not a perfect) option for meat-free eating.

Marshallese is the national language, although **English** has official status and most islanders can speak it as a second language.

Marshallese

I do not eat _____.	Ijjab konnan mona ____.	EE-jahb koh-nahn moh-nah ____.
meat	kaniok	kahn-yohk
chicken	bao	bah-oh
fish	iik	eek
eggs	lib	leeb
Thank you	Kommol	kohm-mohl

Micronesia

The Federated States of Micronesia occupy a large chunk of the western Pacific. The food available depends to a large extent on where you are. In towns, fast food, junk food, and Chinese and American restaurants rule the roost. In more isolated areas, traditional food such as rice, breadfruit, taro, and yams (and of course fish) is more easily available. Unfortunately, junk food is gaining supremacy even in fairly far-flung areas. Hotel and resort restaurants sometimes offer more imaginative dishes, and vegetarian food is often available (especially with advance notice).

English is the official language. Various Micronesian and Polynesian languages are spoken by Micronesians at home.

Nauru

Nauru's one and only product is phosphate. Despite being essentially a mountain of fertilizer, Nauru must import virtually all of its food and most of its fresh water. Needless to say, fresh vegetables are far from plentiful, and food choice is generally restricted to rice or Western-style fast food; there are also a few Chinese restaurants.

Nauruan is the official language, but most Nauruans can speak **English**, which is widely used in commerce and government.

New Zealand

In a country with several times more sheep than people, some of those sheep are bound to get devoured. One might expect New Zealand's cuisine to consist of nothing more than lamb and mutton. However, vegetarianism is surprisingly easy to manage here, even in small communities. The cities and some smaller towns have specialty vegetarian restaurants; in large communities, most standard restaurants offer one or two meatless entrees. (Vegans may have a problem, however, as vegetarian entrees usually contain cheese.) There are also Asian restaurants in the cities, which are more likely to offer vegetarian entrees than their counterparts in Asia. In rural areas, restaurants may not offer meatless dishes; this is not the case in wine-growing areas, where most restaurants will cater to vegetarians. Where restaurants fail, vegetarians will have no problem cooking for themselves, as bulk food stores exist even in small towns.

English is New Zealand's official language. The indigenous Maori speak their own Polynesian language, but usually can also speak English.

The **Cook Islands**, **Tokelau**, and **Niue** are self-governing territories of New Zealand. Their food is generally the Polynesian trio of tubers, fruit, and fish, but more touristed areas offer greater variety and it may even be impossible to get local food. Rarotonga, for example, has many good Western-style restaurants, although not all offer vegetarian entrees. English and Polynesian languages are spoken.

Palau

Palau is a small country of small islands, few people, and limited culinary options. Local cuisine is mostly based on rice, cassava, sweet potatoes, coconuts, and fish. In the towns, there are some Japanese and Chinese restaurants for tourists, as well as western-style fast food. Vegetarian entrees are not commonly offered in the few hotel restaurants.

Both Palauan and **English** are official languages. Other indigenous languages are also spoken.

Papua New Guinea

Papua New Guinea is not a vegetarian paradise. One isolated tribe eats the brains of its dead as a sign of respect (and contracts a malady related to mad cow disease as a result). It is true that you are unlikely to be invited to join in this practice, but other perils await. Strange forest animals are often eaten in the interior. Less mobile traditional cuisine includes sweet potato, taro, sago palm, yam, bananas, and rice. This assortment should be acceptable to vegetarians, but traditional food is difficult to find. Most towns offer only Western-style hamburger joints or Chinese restaurants. (The latter are obviously a better bet for vegetarians.) Port Moresby has a wider variety of eateries, and slightly more sophisticated Western-type food (such as pasta) and Asian cuisines are available. Pesco-vegetarians will find that fish is a staple along the coast and on the outer islands, as well as along major rivers.

There are literally hundreds of Melanesian and Papuan languages spoken in Papua New Guinea. Although **English** is the official language, not everyone speaks it, particularly in the interior. The main medium of intergroup communication, even in fairly remote areas, is **Pidgin**. It should be obvious that Pidgin is derived from English, although most tourists will not be able to understand it.

Pidgin

I would like something without _____.	Mi laik kaikai i no gat _____.	mee lyke kye-kye ee noh gaht _____.
I do not eat _____.	Mi no save kaikai _____.	mee noh sah-vay kye-kye _____.
meat	mit	meet

chicken	kokaruk	koh-kah-rook
fish	pis	pees
eggs	kiau	kee-ow
Thank you	Tenku tru	tehn-kyoo troo

Solomon Islands

Traditional Solomon Islands cuisine is a basic diet of rice, fish, fruit, coconut, beans, and the usual Pacific starches: breadfruit, taro, yam, and sweet potato. Vegetarians can generally find something to eat from this assortment. In towns, Western and Chinese restaurants purvey the usual offerings. Hotel and resort restaurants may occasionally serve vegetarian entrees. Tropical fruit here is widely available and generally outstanding. Chewing betel nut is a common habit in the Solomons; because betel acts as an appetite suppressant, it could be a useful last resort if the available food offerings prove unsatisfactory.

English is the official language. Most inhabitants speak a Melanesian, Papuan, or Polynesian tongue as their first language. **Pijin** can be very useful in parts of the Solomons, and it is often used to bridge local linguistic barriers. Pijin is very similar to Papuan Pidgin, although there are a few differences in usage.

Pijin

I do not eat _____.	Mi no save kaikai _____.	mee noh sah-vay kye-kye _____.
meat	mit	meet
chicken	kokorako	koh-koh-rah-koh
fish	fishi	fee-shee
eggs	egg	ehg
Thank you	Taggio tumas	tah-gyoh too-muhs

Tonga

Traditional Tongan food includes the usual suspects of fish, taro, yams, coconut, breadfruit, bananas and other tropical fruit, pork, and rice. Unfortunately, most restaurants do not serve traditional cuisine. Some "traditional" feasts, which usually target tourists, offer a selection of traditional foods; unfortunately, vegetarians are unlikely to find them particularly attractive, as the centerpiece is usually an imposing array of roast suckling pigs. Western-style restaurants are very common in towns, and sometimes offer vegetarian entrees (although they are more likely to serve fish, chicken, or pork). Chinese and other Asian cuisines are also available.

Both **Tongan** and **English** are official languages.

Tongan

I do not eat _____.	'Oku 'ikai teu kai _____.	OH-koo EE-kye tay-oo kye ____.
meat	kakano'i manu	kah-kh-noh-ee MAH-noo
chicken	moa	moh-wah
fish	ika	EE-kah
eggs	fo'i moa	foh-ee moh-wah
cheese	siisi	see-see
Thank you	Malō	MAH-loh

Tuvalu

Tuvalu is only nine square miles of coral atolls, which have generally poor soil, so most foodstuffs must be imported. As one would expect, variety and freshness are not the watchwords of Tuvaluan food, and processed junk food is the order of the day (with some very limited exceptions, such as breadfruit). You should have no difficulty finding coconut at any rate; it is the main export commodity.

Tuvaluan and **English** are the main languages.

The U.S. Islands

Guam is the most developed of the U.S. Pacific possessions (and of all mid-Pacific islands generally). Guam is "where America's day begins," but that doesn't mean you are guaranteed a decent vegetarian breakfast. American restaurant chains are well represented; there are also many independent restaurants, some of which serve interesting meatless dishes. About a quarter of Guam's population was born in Asia, so Chinese, Japanese, Filipino, and other Asian cuisines are easily available. Guam produces plenty of vegetables, and local markets are good places to enjoy a respite from processed food.

The **Northern Marianas** Islands, stretching north from Guam, are somewhat more traditional and less cosmopolitan than Guam (with the exception of Saipan, which is quite developed).

In both Guam and the Northern Marianas, **English** is treated as the official language, although many islanders speak Chamorro at home.

In **American Samoa**, the traditional fare is like that in Western Samoa—fish, taro, breadfruit, yams, bananas, and coconuts are the main staples. However, Western-style restaurants (and lugubrious fast-food outlets) from the United States are beginning to establish culinary hegemony; it may be difficult to find traditional Samoan food. Most people in American Samoa are bilingual in **Samoan** (p. 233) and **English**.

Assorted other insular American possessions are scattered around the Pacific; most are uninhabited or are used for military purposes, and the authorities are unlikely to welcome vegetarian visitors blundering around.

Vanuatu

Vanuatu offers the usual Pacific island staples of taro, breadfruit, coconut, cassava, and the like. These islands are heavily forested, so an excellent selection of tropical fruits is available. There are also plenty of Western-type cafes and restaurants in the towns, as well as a selection of Chinese restaurants.

English and **French** (p. 66) are both official languages, but various Melanesian languages are spoken in Vanuatuan homes. The most common medium of inter-group communication is Bislama, which is very close to **Pijin** (p. 230) and **Pidgin** (p. 229); those dialects can usually often be understood in Bislama's stead.

Western Samoa

Western Samoa has fertile soil and an excellent climate, resulting in an enticing range of local produce. Traditionally, Samoans have consumed plenty of root vegetables—especially taro root, which is sometimes served with a sauce of coconut cream. Taro leaves are used in traditional dishes. Breadfruit is another starchy staple, and bananas (sometimes cooked and served as a side dish) and other tropical fruit are easily available. However, it is sometimes difficult to find traditional food outside Samoan homes or touristy feasts (beware the obligatory roast suckling pig at the latter). Restaurants and fast-food joints tend to focus on Western fast food and Chinese dishes, although curries and other interesting meatless possibilities can also be found. Pesco-vegetarians will be happy to learn that fish is exceedingly common.

Both **Samoan** and **English** are official languages. Most Samoans are bilingual, although few people speak English in very remote areas, especially on Savaii.

Samoan

I do not eat _____. (polite usage)	Ou te le taumafa i le _____.	oo tay lay tow-MAH-fah ee lay _____.
I do not eat _____. (colloquial usage)	Ou te le ai i le _____.	oo tay lay eye ee lay _____.
meat (generally refers only to beef)	fasi povi	FAH-see POH-vee
pork	fasi pua'a	FAH-see poo-AH-ah
chicken	fasi moa	FAH-see moh-wah
fish	ia	ee-ah
eggs	fua moa	foo-ah moh-wah
cheese	sisi	see-see

I am a vegetarian.
(literally, "I do not eat
the flesh of animals")

Ou te le ai i aano
o manu.

oo tay lay eye ee ah-ah-
noh oh MAH-noo.

Thank you

Faafetai

fah-ah-feh-tye

Index of Languages

Index of Countries and Territories